T0195001

SIMPLY PAUL

the apostle

PATRICK PIETRANTANO

WESTBOW
PRESS®
A DIVISION OF THOMAS NELSON
& ZONDERVAN

WestBow Press books may be ordered through booksellers or by contacting:

WestBow Press
A Division of Thomas Nelson & Zondervan
1663 Liberty Drive
Bloomington, IN 47403
www.westbowpress.com
844-714-3454

Scripture taken from the King James Version of the Bible.

ISBN: 978-1-6642-8748-8 (sc)
ISBN: 978-1-6642-8749-5 (hc)
ISBN: 978-1-6642-8747-1 (e)

Library of Congress Control Number: 2022923649

Print information available on the last page.

WestBow Press rev. date: 02/07/2023

PREFACE

Paul the Apostle? How did he get this knowledge and who gave him such understanding. Paul describes this knowledge as a secret that has never been known to man before. The unveiling of this knowledge to him he describes as a face to face personal experience with Jesus Christ himself. The beginning of his ministry started on the road to Damascus, and the intense conversation that took place with Jesus Christ at that time. You most likely have never heard what took place in that conversation, but it is covered in great detail in this book.

What was the driving motivation that allowed Paul to endure such criticism, beatings and being stoned to death, and brought back from the dead? Demon possession is explained, how it works and how Paul deals with it. Exorcism and exorcists are brought to light in an understanding that will definitely engage you in biblical truth. What truly is an exorcist? You are about to find out!

What took place at the first council in Jerusalem dealing with circumcision and following the law? Was it necessary to observed it be saved or born again? For the Gentile no, but for the Jew they believed it was necessary. You will see the fiery words that took place in those discussions between Paul, the apostles and elders.

The final decision that was determined, was only half right. It was the beginning of a great division that took place in the first century church, and in many churches it still is. The ultimate demise and imprisonment of Paul the Apostle stems from the decisions made at this council. The understanding of this biblical truth has never been captured in any book or commentary that I know of. It will challenge you to discover truths that have been void of understanding.

Why Paul wanted to go to Jerusalem this time will be a heart breaker when you understand what motivated him. When you see all the prophetic words that were spoken to him many times, and especially by a legitimate prophet. What motivated him to disregard and Ignore these words, again it is a heart breaker.

Paul's courteous treatment during his imprisonment and travel to Rome, which for the most part has been a misnomer. Paul's last years in Rome where he penned a lot of the New Testament. It's an adventure of truth that will be enlightening!

At the end of my book I have written:
Pat's poem in a psalm

It is a kind of psalm, a poem and a riddle. I woke up at 3:30 AM and I heard "two years of one" which made no sense to me, but I wrote it down. The rest of it just came to me almost without thinking, it was effortless. It may take some time to figure out what it is about, it did for me. However, let me know what you think. Thank you very much for taking the time to read my book. I am believing it will open new doors of understanding for you. God bless!

patp7757@gmail.com

FOREWORD

I've known Pat Pietrantano for well over 30 years during which time my respect for him has grown immensely both as a personal friend and a dedicated Christian as well as a prolific author. Pat has been involved in biblical research, biblical teaching, as well as counseling for well over a decade. His insight into biblical research and teaching is and has been exemplary. This book on the life and writings of Saul is unique as to the insight into the life of one of the most important authors in the New Testament.

The teachings of Jesus have been exalted above the teaching of the Holy Spirit by Paul as though it was a rivalry between the two. But the words of Christ and the words of Paul are equal in importance in as much as both are recorded and given to us by the same Holy Spirit. After all it was Paul whose surname was Saul who wrote the seven Church epistles which the Holy Spirit addressed are Romans, Corinthians, Galatians, Ephesians, Philippians, Colossians, and the Thessalonians. That is the same number of Asian churches that Christ himself addressed in revelations 2 and 3. These epistles contain the ABCs of Christian instructions for us today. Unfortunately they are very seldom taught in the churches of today.

Mr. Pietrantano has captured the whole emphasis of the life of Paul in a unique format that every Christian should read and study. I am convinced that Mr. Pietrantano Was inspired by the same Holy Spirit that led Paul throughout his ministry.

Reverend William F Pfeiffer.

CONTENTS

CHAPTER 1

Paul's Road to Damascus

Saul was born in Tarsus, a city in the province of Cilicia in what today is called Turkey in Asia Minor. He was born about AD 4, in the same time period when Jesus Christ was born about 2 BC. Saul was educated in Jerusalem at the feet of Gamaliel and was taught according to the prefect manner of the law. This was Paul's statement the day he was taken prisoner in Jerusalem:

> I am verily a man which am a Jew, born in Tarsus, a city in Cilicia, yet brought up in this city at the feet of Gamaliel and taught according to the perfect manner of the law of the fathers, and was zealous toward God, as ye are all this day. (Acts 22:3)

We would refer to Paul's education today as PhD level. Gamaliel was a well-respected rabbi among all Jews, and a doctor of the Law. There is more about Gamaliel's judgments later in Acts:

> Then stood there up one in the council, a Pharisee, named Gamaliel, a doctor of the law, had a reputation

among all the people, and commanded to put the apostles forth little space. (Acts 5:34)

Gamaliel introduced great understanding in the minds of the high priest and the Sadducees when they tried to kill the apostles in Acts 5. You have to ask? Was Saul at that council meeting when his professor, Gamaliel, gave his insight, or did Saul at least hear about it? Whichever way it went, Paul did not follow the guidance of his teacher. It's a great record in the Word of God. Take some time and read Acts 5:12–42.

The first time Saul shows up is in Acts 7, so let's begin.

And cast him [Stephen] out of the city, and stoned him, and the witnesses laid down their clothes at a young man's feet, whose name is Saul. And they stoned Stephen, calling upon God, and saying, Lord Jesus, receive my spirit. And he kneeled down, and cried with a loud voice, Lord, lay not this sin to their charge. And when he had said this, he fell asleep. (Acts 7:58–60)

And Saul was consenting unto his death. And at that time there was great persecution against the church which was at Jerusalem; and they were all scattered abroad throughout the regions of Judaea and Samaria, except the apostles. (Acts 8:1)

Saul, in chapter 8 of the book of Acts, was there at the stoning of Stephen. Saul heard and was witness to the accusations against Stephen:

And set up false witnesses, which said, this man ceaseth not to speak blasphemous words against this holy place, and the law: For we have heard him say, that this Jesus of Nazareth shall destroy this place, and shall change the customs which Moses delivered us. (Acts 6:13–14)

In the seventh chapter of Acts, Stephen presented the genetic lineage from Abraham to the Just One (Jesus) and called these false witnesses betrayers and murderers:

> Ye stiffnecked and uncircumcised in heart and ears, ye do always resist the Holy Ghost: as your fathers did, so do ye. Which of the prophets have not your fathers persecuted? And they have slain them which shewed before of the coming of the Just One; of whom ye have been now the betrayers and murderers. (Acts 7: 51-52)

After the stoning of Stephen, Saul was consenting unto Stephen's death:

> And at that time there was a great persecution against the church which was at Jerusalem; and they were all scattered abroad throughout the regions of Judaea and Samaria, except the apostles. (Acts 8:1)

Acts 8:1 says, "And Saul was consenting unto his [Stephen's] death." The word "consenting" is important to understand. As a noun, "consent" means giving permission for something to happen or agreement to do something. As a verb, "to consent" means to give permission for something to happen. Saul began his attack and persecution of believers in Jerusalem and scattered them throughout the regions, as recorded in Galatians:

> For ye have heard of my conversation in times past in the Jew's religion, how that beyond measure I persecuted the church of God, and wasted it. (1:13)

Acts 9 begins with Saul's acknowledgment of his threats and slaughter against the disciples of the Lord. Saul went to the high priest for confirmation and approval to do more of the same in Damascus:

> And Saul, yet breathing out threatening and slaughter against the disciples of the Lord, went to the high priest. And desired of him letters to Damascus to the synagogues, that if he found any of this way, whether they were men or women, he might bring them bound to Jerusalem. (Acts 9:1–2)

Saul at this point was a man of total conviction. His faith was in Judaism. He believed he was serving God by cleansing Judaism of the new way of this Jesus, who was supposed to be the Messiah.

Looking into the mind of Saul, who was a Pharisee and a member of the Sanhedrin, the ruling body of Israel, I have to ask some questions. Was he there when the Pharisees accused Jesus throughout the gospels? Was he at the trial of Jesus when He stood before the high priest? The Word of God does not tell us. Surely Saul must have heard about the miracles that the man Jesus did.

Saul was on his way to Damascus when a light from heaven shone around him and he fell to earth:

> And as he journeyed, he came near Damascus: and suddenly there shined round about him a light from heaven: And he fell to the earth, and heard a voice saying unto him, Saul, Saul, why persecutes me? And he said, who art thou Lord? And the Lord said, I am Jesus whom thou persecutes: it is hard for thee to kick against the pricks. (Acts 9: 3-5)

Astonishingly this was not all that Jesus said to Saul at that time, but these are the only words that are recorded here in Acts 9. To understand the whole conversation, we have to look at the record in Acts 26. This was Paul's statement made to King Agrippa when Paul was taken prisoner in Jerusalem and held in Caesarea for two years, before he was taken to Rome:

> Whereupon as I went to Damascus with authority and commission from the chief priests. At midday, O king, I saw in the way a light from heaven, above the brightness of the sun, shining round about me and them which journeyed with me. And when we were all fallen to the earth, I heard a voice speaking unto me, and saying in the Hebrew tongue, Saul, Saul, why persecutest thou me? It is hard for thee to kick against the pricks. And I said, who art thou, Lord? And he said, I am Jesus whom thou persecutest. But rise, and stand upon thy feet: for I have appeared unto thee for this purpose, to make thee a minister and a witness both of these things which thou hast seen, and of those things in which I will appear unto thee. Delivering thee from the people, and from the Gentiles, unto whom now I send thee. To open their eyes, and to turn them from darkness to light, and from the power of Satan unto God, that they may receive forgiveness of sins, and inheritance among them which are sanctified by faith that is in me. (Acts26:12–18)

After reading and understanding the whole conversation that took place, can you imagine what was going through Saul's mind? Let's consider what Jesus told Saul. Acts 26 says that Jesus appeared to Saul for these purposes:

- to make Saul a minister and a witness of the things he had seen
- to make Saul a witness of those things in which Jesus would appear to him again
- to deliver Saul from the people (Jews) and the Gentiles to whom Jesus is sending him
- to open the people's eyes and turn them from darkness to light, and from the power of Satan to God, that they may receive forgiveness of sins and an inheritance by the sanctifying acts of Jesus himself

Again, if you understand what took place on that day, it changes your whole perspective. This was not a short conversation Jesus had with Saul. Saul was terrified, trembling, and astonished. He asked Jesus, "What do you want me to do?"

> Jesus simply said, "Arise, and go into the city, and it shall be told thee what thou must do" (Acts 9:6).

What anticipation Paul must have experienced, knowing that Jesus was going to appear to him again and talk with him. "What will Jesus say? What will Jesus have to tell me?"

What a road trip that was! Can you imagine what Saul was experiencing at that time? Everything Saul had known about God was through the Law of Moses. Then he was told by Jesus that he was going to be a minister and a witness for Jesus, plus to expect other appearances from Him. Moreover, Jesus wanted Saul to go to the Gentiles. Going to the Gentiles had not been permitted even during Jesus's earthly ministry. When Jesus sent the seventy disciples out, He explicitly told them *not* to go to the Gentiles. There had to have been conflict in Saul's mind.

Jesus also told Saul that he had to realize the people he had been persecuting and killing was Jesus Himself: "Saul, Saul, why persecutest thou me?" The people Saul was killing were Jesus's body.

When Saul got up, he was blind. The men who were with him led him by his hand to Damascus, where he was three days without sight. He did not eat or drink anything. What a time of reflection and meditation upon the contrast between the Word of God that Saul knew, versus the words Jesus had just spoken to him. Saul was well educated in scripture. He described himself as:

> "circumcised the eighth day, of the stock of Israel, of the tribe of Benjamin, a Hebrew of the Hebrews; as touching the law, a pharisee" (Philippians 3:5).

We also know Saul prayed in the house of Judas (not Iscariot) while he was blind. This was the house the men took Paul to, on a street called straight in Damascus. During those three days, Saul had a vision of a man named Ananias coming in and laying his hands on him. When Ananias came in and ministered to Saul, Saul regained his sight and began to preach in the synagogue that Jesus is the Christ, the son of God.

> And Ananias went his way and entered into the house; and putting his hands on him said, brother Saul, the Lord even Jesus that appeared unto thee in the way as thou camest, hath sent me, that thou mightest receive thy sight, and be filled with the Holy Ghost. And immediately there fell from his eyes as it had been scales, and he received his sight forthwith, and arose and was baptized. And when he had received meat, he was strengthened. Then was Saul certain days with the disciples which were at Damascus. And straightway he preached Christ in the synagogues, that he is the son of God. (Acts 9:17–20)

This was the origin of the apostle Paul, whose name was Saul. He received the great revelation, called *the mystery*, that fulfilled the Word of God:

> Whereof I am made a minister according to the dispensation of God which is given to me for you, to fulfill the word of God. Even the mystery which hath been hid from ages and from generations, but now is made manifest to his saints. To whom God would make known what is the riches of the glory of this mystery among the Gentiles; which is Christ in you, the hope of glory. (Colossians 1:25–27)

CHAPTER 2

The Journey Begins

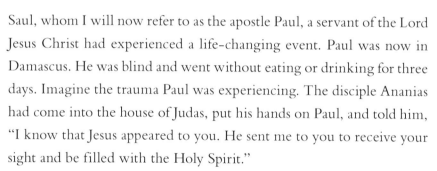

Saul, whom I will now refer to as the apostle Paul, a servant of the Lord Jesus Christ had experienced a life-changing event. Paul was now in Damascus. He was blind and went without eating or drinking for three days. Imagine the trauma Paul was experiencing. The disciple Ananias had come into the house of Judas, put his hands on Paul, and told him, "I know that Jesus appeared to you. He sent me to you to receive your sight and be filled with the Holy Spirit."

Let's talk for a moment about Ananias. The Word of God says he was a disciple, not an apostle, prophet, evangelist, pastor, or teacher. He was simply a believer in Jesus Christ. In Acts 9 we see the conversation the Lord had with Ananias and the conversation Ananias had with the Lord.

> And there was a certain disciple at Damascus named Ananias, and to him said the Lord in a vision, Ananias, and he said, behold I am here Lord. And the Lord said unto him, Arise, and go to the street which is called straight, and enquire in the house of Judas for one called

Saul of Tarsus, for behold he prayeth. And hath seen in a vision a man named Ananias coming in and putting his hands on him that he might receive his sight. Then Ananias answered, Lord, I have heard by many about this man, how much evil he hath done to thy saints at Jerusalem. And here he hath authority from the chief priests to bind all that call on thy name. But the Lord said unto him. Go thy way; for he is a chosen vessel unto me, to bear my name before the Gentiles and kings, and the children of Israel. (Acts 9: 9–15)

Clearly Ananias wanted to remind the Lord about this character Saul, who had a very brutal reputation for persecuting believers in Jesus. One can imagine Ananias saying, are you telling me this man is here in Damascus? And you want me to what? I feel this point is very important. In our conversations with the Lord, we must be honest and open, as Ananias was. God will not be offended by our questions He is expecting questions from us. After the Lord explained, Ananias trusted, obeyed, and did what the Lord asked him to do. He was a great help in the start of the ministry of a great man of God, the apostle Paul.

The men who led Paul by the hand to Damascus and to the Jews, told the whole story of what had just happened. They knew that Paul was not a *follower of the way*. This was what people who believed that Jesus was the Christ, the Son of God, were called at that time. When Ananias came to the house of Judas, Ananias was exposing himself as one of those people. It took great courage, because believers at that time were being hunted and killed. I can't help but imagine what Judas and the members of his household thought when Ananias walked in and ministered to Saul. Were the Jews in Damascus told how Saul regained his sight? These were the people who were going to help Saul persecute believers in Damascus.

After Saul received his miracle, he began to teach that this Jesus was the Christ, the Anointed One, the Son of God. The Jews in Damascus took counsel to kill Paul. How the tables had turned. In a very short time, it got so bad in Damascus that at night the disciples had to help Paul escape in a basket over the city wall.

> But Saul increased the more in strength, and confounded the Jews which dwelt at Damascus, proving that this is the very Christ. And after that many days were fulfilled, the Jews took council to kill him. But their laying await was known of Saul, and they watched the gates day and night to kill him. Then the disciples took him by night, and let him down by the wall in a basket. (Acts 9:22–25)

Question: What passages from the Old Testament do you think Saul was using to prove to the Jews in Damascus that Jesus is the Christ? Just asking!

The next time line needs to be understood correctly. Saul returned to Jerusalem after the Damascus encounter, but only for a short time:

> And when Saul was come to Jerusalem, he assayed to join himself to the disciples, but they were afraid of him, and believed not that he was a disciple. (Acts 9:26)

Barnabas took Paul to the apostles and explained what Paul had done in Damascus:

> But Barnabas took him and brought him to the apostles, and declared unto them how he hath seen the Lord in the way, and that He had spoken to him, and how he had preached boldly at Damascus in the name of Jesus. And he was with them coming in and going out at

Jerusalem. And he spake boldly in the name of the Lord Jesus, and disputed against the Grecians but they went about to slay him. (Acts 9:27–29)

What did Paul say to the Jews at Jerusalem that they wanted to kill him? He was passionate. Jesus had appeared to him, and the experience had changed his life. He spoke boldly! We might get the same results when people get offended about Jesus.

A detailed explanation of this short time Paul was in Jerusalem can be found in Acts 22. This record gives an accurate explanation of what Paul received in a vision from the Lord during this short time he was in Jerusalem:

> And it came to pass, that when I came again to Jerusalem, even when I prayed in the temple, I was in a trance. (vision) And saw Him saying unto me; make haste, and get thee quickly out of Jerusalem, for they will not receive thy testimony concerning me. And I said, Lord, they know that I imprisoned and beat in every synagogue them that believe on thee. And when the blood of thy martyr Stephen was shed, I also was standing by, and consenting unto his death, and kept the raiment of them that slew him. And He said to me; Depart: for I will send thee far hence unto the Gentiles. (Acts 22:17–21)

After leaving Jerusalem from the advice of the Lord, Paul spent a short time in his hometown Tarsus, possibly checking in with family before his journey to Arabia.

> When the brethren knew, they brought him down to Caesarea, and sent him forth to Tarsus. (Acts 9: 30)

Paul now explains what he received in Arabia from Jesus Christ.

Let's go to the epistle to the Galatians and see what Paul recorded about these events:

> But I certify you brethren, that the gospel which was preached of me is not after man. For I neither received it of man, neither was I taught it, but by the revelation of Jesus Christ. For ye have heard of my conversation in time past in the Jews religion, how that beyond measure I persecuted the church of God and wasted it. And profited in the Jews religion above many equals in mine nation, being more exceedingly zealous of the traditions of my fathers. But when it pleased God, who separated me from my mother's womb, and called me by his grace. To reveal his son in me, that I might preach him among the heathen; immediately I conferred not with flesh and blood. Neither went I up to Jerusalem to them which were apostles before me; but I went into Arabia, and returned again unto Damascus. Then after three years I went up to Jerusalem to see Peter, and abode with him fifteen days. (Galatians 1:11–18)

The Message Bible translation of verse 12 gives us a better understanding of the further appearances Jesus had with Paul in Arabia:

> "I got it straight from God. I received the message directly from Jesus Christ." He was not led to get counsel from the apostles!

Paul spent three years in Arabia. Where did he go specifically and why? What Paul received by revelation from Jesus Christ during those three years coincided with what he taught, and collided with Jewish thought and the Law. Paul was told not to go to the apostles. The apostles ministered to Jews only at that time. Jesus's ministry when He was here on earth was to Jews only. His sacrificial life that He gave on the cross was for the world. Paul was receiving detailed revelation about what Jesus accomplished for the believer.

The Word of God does not give us any definite locations in Arabia. This three-year period was about the same amount of time Jesus spent with the twelve apostles when He was on earth. Some think Paul spent time in Petra. Petra was at that time controlled by the Nebatean culture. I too believe Paul spent some time there. However, Paul's ultimate destination was Mount Sinai in Arabia where God gave Moses the Ten Commandments. How appropriate is that? As Paul states in Galatians 1:12 in the Good News translation,

> "I did not receive it from any human being, nor did anyone teach it to me. It was Jesus Christ himself who revealed to me."

Jesus Christ revealed to Paul that He, Jesus Christ, was the end of the Law. Jew and Gentile were made one in the body of Christ, and there was no difference between them. Christ Himself lives in each believer.

The next revelation that Jesus taught Paul was that this body of Christ would be gathered together, what some refer to as *the rapture*. This gathering together will happen before what the prophets of old foretold of the dark and terrible day of the Lord, which is the seven years of the tribulation period. This was the first time the revelation of the body of Christ and the gathering together was revealed. It had been kept secret from the foundation of the world. Jesus assigned these revelations to Paul to teach the world the purpose for which He came. As we will see, Paul was persecuted greatly for it.

For Christ is the end of the law for righteousness to everyone that believeth. (Romans 10:4)

For he is our peace, who hath made both one, and hath broken down the middle wall of partition between us. (Ephesians 2:14–16)

What a verse! Christ is the end of the Law; that says it all. Righteousness comes by believing, not by works. Both Jew and Gentile are made one in the body of Christ.

The veil in the Temple was torn in two at the death of Christ, signifying that we now have direct access to the Father, both Jew and Gentile. God Himself tore that veil. The separation has ceased. There is no difference anymore.

Having abolished in his flesh the enmity, even the law of commandments contained in ordinances, for to make in himself of twain one new man, so making peace. And that he might reconcile both unto God in one body by the cross, having slain the enmity thereby. (Ephesians 2:15–16)

Having therefore, brethren, boldness to enter into the holiest by the blood of Jesus, by a new and living way, which he hath consecrated for us, THROUGH THE VEIL, that is to say, his flesh. (Hebrews 10:19–20)

Now we beseech you brethren, by the coming of our Lord Jesus Christ, and by our gathering together unto him. That ye be not soon shaken in mind, or be troubled, neither by spirit, nor by word, nor by letter as from us, as that the day of Christ is at hand. Let no man deceive you by any means; for that day shall not come, except there come a falling away first, and that man of sin be revealed, the son of perdition. (2 Thessalonians 2:1–3)

These truths that Jesus taught Paul were the first time anybody heard them. They were a foreign thought to Jewish belief, even to the apostles. Do you think Paul's eyes were beginning to open, as promised by Jesus Himself during Paul's Damascus experience?

Paul's three years in Arabia were spent with Jesus. Paul wrote in his church epistles what Jesus taught him, which is the covenant of the New Testament that was paid for by the blood of Jesus. Paul learned directly from Jesus what he would teach and write in his epistles to the body of Christ. What a three-year sabbatical that must have been! It's very possible that Paul was in the very cleft of the rock where God told Moses to hide himself on Mount Sinai, where Moses received the Ten Commandments. God showed Moses His back side; Jesus showed Paul His whole side and what Jesus paid for with the sacrifice of His body.

> In the body of his flesh through death, to present you holy and unblameable and unreproveable in his sight. (Colossians 1:22)

Is this how you see yourself in His sight? If not, why not? What do we as born-again believers really have inside? Are you ready? It is Christ in you, the hope of glory! Is that really true? Can we possibly do what Jesus did when He walked on this earth?

> Verily, verily, I say unto you, he that believeth on me, the works that I do shall he do also; and greater works than these shall he do, because I go to my father. (John 14:12)

In most churches today, that statement would be considered blasphemous, demonstrating extreme pride and a lack of humility. But that is exactly what Jesus said we must be doing.

Now that stretches my faith. It makes me uncomfortable and unconfident. When we look at our own inadequacies, every negative thought comes charging into our minds: That can't be true or I am just not good enough. If we don't understand who we are in Christ Jesus, what I call our sonship rights, we allow condemning thoughts to have dominance over what Jesus said and how Jesus revealed it to the apostle Paul in Arabia. Then the words we read in His Word will not work in our lives. It is a decision we all have to make. We must either be content with certain church doctrine, or be bold and believe what Jesus said, and revealed to Paul.

CHAPTER 3

Transitional Times

During the period when Paul was in Arabia, receiving the great revelation of the mystery from Jesus Christ, the main character in the book of Acts changed to Peter. In Acts 9, Peter healed a man named Aeneas, who had been sick for eight years with palsy. Later in this same chapter, Peter raised a woman named Dorcas from the dead:

> And it came to pass, as Peter passed throughout all quarters, he came down also to the saints which dwelt at Lydda. And there he found a certain man named Aeneas, which had kept his bed eight years, and was sick of the palsy. And Peter said unto him, Aeneas, Jesus Christ maketh thee whole: arise, and make thy bed. And he arose immediately. (Acts 9:32–34)

Next, two disciples were sent to get Peter because a woman named Dorcas had died. They were expecting Peter to raise her from the dead. These disciples believed in the power of God.

And forasmuch as Lydda was nigh to Joppa, and the disciples had heard that Peter was there, they sent unto him two men, desiring him that he would not delay to come to them. Then Peter arose and went with them. When he was come, they brought him into the upper chamber: and all the widows stood by him weeping, and shewing the coats and garments which Dorcas made, while she was with them. But Peter put them all forth, and kneeled down, and prayed, and turning him to the body said, Tabitha, arise. And she opened her eyes: and when she saw Peter, she sat up. And he gave her his hand, and lifted her up, and when he called the saints and widows, presented her alive. (Acts 9:38–41)

Praise God! Miracles were happening; people were being healed and raised from the dead.

Then God started moving Peter in a different direction with a vision that confused Peter. It introduced a new thought about God and how God was about to operate in this new administration. God was trying to teach Peter the same things Paul was undergoing in Arabia, and it was a hard thing to swallow for Peter. The record begins in Acts 10 and is completed in Acts 11:

There was a certain man in Caesarea called Cornelius, a centurion of the band called the Italian band … He saw in a vision evidently about the ninth hour of the day, an angel of God coming unto him, and saying unto him, Cornelius. … And now send men to Joppa, and call for one Simon, whose surname is Peter. He lodgeth with one Simon a tanner, whose house is by the sea side: he shall tell thee what thou oughtest to do. (Acts 10:1, 3, 5–6)

Cornelius was a Gentile and a centurion in the Roman army, called the Italian band. He lived in Caesarea, where he had a visitation from an angel of God. Cornelius received very specific instructions from the angel on where to go and who to look for.

The next day, Peter went on the rooftop and saw a vision:

> On the morrow, as they went on their journey, and drew nigh unto the city, Peter went up upon the housetop to pray about the sixth hour. And he became very hungry, and would have eaten, but while they made ready, he fell into a trance. (vision) And saw heaven opened, and a certain vessel descending unto him, as it had been a great sheet knit at the four corners, and let down to the earth. Wherein were all manner of four-footed beasts of the earth, and wild beasts, and creeping things, and fowls of the air. And there came a voice to him, rise Peter, kill and eat. But Peter said, not so Lord, for I have never eaten anything that is common or unclean. And the voice spake unto him again the second time, what God hath cleansed, that call not thou common. This was done trice, and the vessel was received up again into heaven. (Acts 10:9–16)

Peter had heard that voice before on the Mount of Transfiguration with James and John, when Jesus was transfigured before their eyes and spoke to Moses and Elijah. But this time Peter said no to the Lord. The animals in his vision were unclean, not kosher for a Jew to eat. So why was God telling him to eat? Peter was in a dilemma, not understanding what was being communicated to him. It seemed to be a direct contradiction of the Law and what Moses taught. Moreover, Jesus followed the Law and never ate anything unclean.

After the vessel went back up into the heavens, Peter was still on the rooftop, doubting what the vision meant:

> Now while Peter doubted in himself, what this vision which he hath seem should mean, behold the men which were sent from Cornelius had made inquiry for Simon's house, and stood before the gate … While Peter thought on the vision, the spirit said unto him, behold three men seek thee. Arise therefore, and get thee down, and go with them doubting nothing, for I have sent them. (Acts 10:17, 19–20)

God had great timing, trying to help Peter understand. Peter knew it was unlawful for a Jew to have anything to do with Gentiles, but God had shown Peter not to call any man common or unclean. Peter went to Caesarea and entered Cornelius's house, where Cornelius's kinsmen and friends were waiting. What was the first thing Peter said?

> And he said unto them, ye know how that it is an unlawful thing for a man that is a Jew to keep company, or come unto one of another nation; but God hath showed me that I should not call any man common or unclean. (Acts 10:28)

At the end of Peter's talk, the Holy Spirit fell on them all at Cornelius's house:

> While Peter yet spake these words, the Holy Ghost fell on all them which heard the word. And they of the circumcision which believed were astonished, as many as came with Peter, because that on the Gentiles also was poured out the gift of the Holy Ghost. For they

heard them speak with tongues, and magnify God. (Acts 10:44–46)

The other Jews who believed and came with Peter were astonished. Why were they astonished? Because the Gentiles also received the gift of the Holy Spirit. How did the Jews recognize that? Because they heard the Gentiles speak in tongues and magnify God. Peter and the other Jews who believed could not deny this evidence. This was what Jesus was teaching Paul in Arabia. Peter was learning it in the physical realm. This became a major issue for the church at Jerusalem, as we will see later in Acts.

Peter was criticized for speaking God's Word to Gentiles when he went back to Jerusalem, so he rehearsed the matter and explained:

> And when Peter was come up to Jerusalem, they that were of the circumcision contended with him. Saying, thou wentest in to men uncircumcised, and did eat with them. But Peter rehearsed the matter from the beginning, and expounded it by order unto them. (Acts 11:2–4)

At the end of his explanation, he added:

> Forasmuch then as God gave them the like gift as he did unto us, who believed on the Lord Jesus Christ; what was I, that I could withstand God? When they heard these things, they held their peace, and glorified God, saying, Then hath God also to the Gentiles granted repentance unto life. (Acts 11:17–18)

This record of Peter with Cornelius occurred about AD 40, approximately eight to ten years after the initial pouring out of the Holy Ghost on Pentecost, as described in Acts 2. When these Gentiles spoke in tongues, it was proof that Gentiles were granted repentance unto life. However, the mystery of the one body had not yet been revealed by Paul.

Understanding of this time period between Passover and Pentecost is essential, and where the original outpouring of the Holy Ghost in Acts 2 took place.

There is a fifty-day period between Passover and Pentecost. We know Jesus died on Passover and rose from the dead three days later, on the Feast of First Fruits. That left forty-seven days until Pentecost. Jesus Christ was alive on this planet in His resurrected body for forty days. At the end of those forty days was His ascension into heaven. So from His ascension to Pentecost was a seven-day period, not ten. I understand that this seven-day period goes against certain theological teaching, but you can't deny the facts as they are laid out.

Where did this outpouring of the Holy Spirit in Acts 2 take place, in the upper room or in the house? Commentaries and all teaching that I have read place this event in the upper room. Let's allow the Word to speak for itself:

> And when the day of Pentecost was fully come, they were all with one accord in one place. And suddenly there came a sound from heaven as of a rushing mighty wind, and it filled all the house where they were sitting. (Acts 2:1–2)

The words "house" and "temple" are synonymous throughout the Bible. From the house that Solomon built for the Lord, which was the Temple, to the incident when Jesus threw the moneychangers out of the Temple:

> And he went into the temple, and began to cast out them that sold therein, and them that bought. Saying

unto them, it is written, my house is the house of prayer,
but you have made it a den of thieves. (Luke 19:45–46)

So where was Jesus when He cast the moneychangers out? Was it a house or the Temple? The words are synonymous. They are the same place! This truth is very simple, yet it has not been taught accurately, and it should be. Another fact is that the same Greek word is used in Acts 2 and Luke 19. Of a certainty, the great gift of the Holy Spirit was given to the world on the day of Pentecost in God's own house, the Temple. This was the birth of the church, the body of Christ, and God celebrated the birth of His children in His house, *the Temple*. This is such a simple truth, and yet religious teaching has been the dominant thought.

CHAPTER 4

After Arabia

In the later part of Acts 11, we see the believers who were scattered or ran for their lives from Saul after the stoning of Stephen in Jerusalem. They went to Phenice, which is in modern-day Lebanon; Cyprus, which is an island in the Mediterranean Sea off the coast of Turkey; and Antioch, a city in Syria. They preached the Word to Jews only.

> Now they which were scattered abroad upon the persecution that arose about Stephen, travelled as far as Phenice, and Cyprus, and Antioch, preaching the word to none but unto the Jews only. Some of them were men of Cyprus and Cyrene, which when they were come to Antioch, spake unto the Grecians, preaching the Lord Jesus. (Acts 11:19–20)

However, some preached the Lord Jesus to the Gentiles, which was unheard of at this time. Many Gentiles believed. The church at Jerusalem heard about this and sent Barnabas to investigate.

Then tidings of these things came unto the ears of the church which was at Jerusalem; and they sent forth Barnabas, that he should go as far as Antioch. (Acts 11:22)

Perhaps Peter's experience at Cornelius's house was an isolated incident, and not the direction God intended.

Barnabas recognized the grace of God in that Jews were allowed by God to speak now to Gentiles about the Lord Jesus and be born again. I believe Barnabas was in Jerusalem when Peter returned from Cornelius's house, and Barnabas heard the whole story as Peter told it.

For he was a good man, and full of the Holy Ghost and of faith. And much people was added unto the Lord. Then departed Barnabas to Tarsus, to seek Paul. (Acts 11:24–25)

Barnabas remembered what Jesus told Paul: "I am sending you to the Gentiles." Barnabas immediately went to find Paul and inform him about what was happening with the Gentiles. I believe Barnabas was led by the Holy Spirit to seek Saul, who by this time had become the apostle Paul after returning from Arabia. Tarsus was where Paul was born. Apparently, Barnabas knew that and found Paul at Tarsus. Perhaps Paul came back to Tarsus after returning from Mount Sinai in Arabia, to see family and check in before starting his ministry journeys.

If we do the math correctly, the time between Passover, when Moses led the children of Israel out of Egypt, to the point when God gave Moses the Ten Commandments was about fifty days. The giving of the Ten Commandments correlates with the timing of Pentecost. What a contrast between how God used Pentecost to give the Law to Moses in one era and gave Paul an entirely different revelation on Mount Sinai centuries later.

"The day of Pentecost was fully come" (Acts 2:1).

Not only had Pentecost fully come, but the other three spring feasts were also fully come: Passover, Unleavened Bread, and First Fruits.

- *Passover* represents the crucifixion and death of the Lord Jesus Christ.
- *Unleavened Bread* involves eating bitter herbs and bread made without yeast, representing the burial and the bitter taste of the death of Jesus Christ.
- *First Fruits* represents Jesus Christ's resurrection from the dead.
- *Pentecost* is the giving of the Holy Spirit, the birth of God's own children. The Holy Spirit is the seed of God Himself; that's why receiving the Holy Spirit is called being *born again*.

This was given to the apostle Paul, called the administration of grace, the church age. For the most part his revelation has been drowned out by religious teaching. The truth is that every believer has perfect standing before God in Christ. We have been made righteous, not by our works but by his work.

> For he [God] hath made him [Jesus] to be sin for us, who knew no sin, that we might be made the righteousness of God in him. (2 Corinthians 5:21)

Every believer is justified. *Justified* means it is as though you have never sinned.

> And by him, all that believe are justified from all things, from which ye could not be justified by the law of Moses. (Acts 13:39).

The truth of this revelation has to be recaptured in our understanding, if the body of Christ is to walk in the power and authority given to us by the body of His flesh:

> For it pleased the Father that in him should all fulness dwell. And having made peace through the blood of his cross, by him to reconcile all things unto himself; by him I say, whether they be things in earth, or things in heaven. And you, that were sometime alienated and enemies in your mind by wicked works, yet now hath he reconciled. In the body of his flesh, through death, to present you, holy and unblameable and unreproveable in his sight. (Colossians 1:19–22)

Paul received the revelation of this administration or dispensation of the age of grace that is so misunderstood even today. Paul was given the responsibility by Jesus to teach the administration change from Law to grace. The revelation of this great mystery has been sterilized by the so-called Christian church. Preparation for death and judgment has replaced the great hope of the blessed return of Christ for His body.

Paul and Barnabas returned to Antioch to teach:

> And when he [Barnabas] had found him, [Paul] he brought him unto Antioch. And it came to pass, that a whole year they assembled themselves with the church, and taught the people. And the disciples were called christians first in Antioch. (Acts 11:26).

What was Paul teaching? He was teaching what he had been taught in Arabia by Jesus:

Whereof I am made a minister, according to the dispensation of God which is given to me, for you, to fulfill the word of God. Even the mystery which hath been hid from ages and from generations, but now is made manifest to his saints. To whom God would make known what is the riches of the glory of this mystery, among the Gentiles, which is Christ in you, the hope of glory. (Colossians 1:25–27)

The revelation Paul received fulfilled the word of God. That statement is virtually unheard of in any church today. What do you think the believers in Antioch were telling everybody? It's Christ in me! Sin, sickness, and disease are canceled in my life and in my body. That is what Jesus did when He was here on earth. Now He is in me, and we can do the same as He did.

The last part of verse 26 in Acts 11 says the disciples "were called Christians first in Antioch." The church is the body of Christ, not a building. That must be understood. Most people have no idea where the word Christian comes from. The term Christian is used ignorantly today. It's been desecrated and is void of understanding of its true meaning. The believers in Antioch were telling everybody what Paul was teaching: "It's Christ in me." Get it? Christ-in or Christian, take out the A and you've got it. This revelation Paul taught in Antioch is where the word Christian originated.

CHAPTER 5

The Other Antioch

Next in the book of Acts, God sends a prophet named Agabus from Jerusalem to Antioch:

> And in these days came prophets from Jerusalem unto Antioch. And there stood up one of them named Agabus, and signified by the spirit that there should be great dearth throughout all the world; which came to pass in the days of Claudius Caesar. (Acts 11:27–28)

Agabus needs to be recognized here as a true, legitimate prophet. The prophecy given by Agabus in Antioch to the body of Christ was to prepare, because a food shortage was coming. His prophecy came to pass as a sign of his legitimacy. Later in Acts, when Agabus gave his prophecy to the apostle Paul, it was again a warning to Paul not to go to Jerusalem.

Claudius Caesar reigned as emperor of Rome from AD 41 to 54. Josephus affirmed this famine in his history, saying it hit Rome, Greece, Egypt, and Judea from AD 44 to 48. This time frame coincided with the death of Herod in AD 44, recorded in Acts 12:

And upon a set day Herod, arrayed in royal apparel sat upon his throne, and made an oration unto them. And the people gave a shout, saying, it is the voice of a god, and not man. And immediately the angel of the Lord smote him, because he gave not God the glory; and he was eaten of worms, and gave up the ghost. (Acts 12:21–23)

In the same year, AD 44, Herod murdered the apostle James, brother of John the apostle, and put Peter in prison, planning to murder him too:

Now about the time Herod the king stretched forth his hands to vex certain of the church. And he killed James the brother of John with the sword. And because he saw it pleased the Jews, he proceeded further to take Peter also. Then were days of unleavened bread. (Acts 12:1–3)

Herod is a title, much like governor or mayor, and not a proper name. This Herod was Herod Agrippa 1, the grandson of Herod the Great. The murder of James occurred in the spring of AD 44, for it was the feast day of unleavened bread, the week of Passover. This Herod's reign was very short, AD 41–44, because of his vicious murder of the apostle James.

The disciples sent relief to their brethren in Judaea by the hands of Barnabas and Paul: Then the disciples, every man according to his ability, determined to send relief unto the brethren which dwelt in Judaea. Which also they did, and sent it to the elders by the hands of Barnabas and Saul. (Acts 11:29–30)

Here is a thought that needs to be considered:

Believers under the teaching of Paul and Barnabas in Antioch had more than enough even during the famine to send relief to the churches in Jerusalem and Judaea.

When Barnabas and Paul return to Antioch from Jerusalem, they brought John-Mark with them:

> And Barnabas and Saul returned from Jerusalem, when they had fulfilled their ministry, and took with them John, whose surname was Mark. (Acts 12:25)

> Now there were in the church that was at Antioch prophets and teachers, as Barnabas, and Simon that was called Niger, and Lucius of Cyrene, and Manaen, which had been brought up with Herod the tetrarch, and Saul. As they ministered to the Lord, and fasted, the Holy Ghost said, separate me Barnabas and Saul for the work whereunto I have called them. (Acts 13:1–2)

We have to understand how the gifts of the Spirit work. This prophecy regarding Barnabas and Saul was given by Barnabas himself: "separate me Barnabas and Saul for the work." They took John, whose surname was Mark, to be their minister. John-Mark was the author of the gospel of Mark and was described as the son of a woman named Mary:

> And when he had considered the thing, he [Peter] came to the house of Mary the mother of John, who's surname was Mark, where many were gathered together praying. (Acts 12:12)

This was the house that Peter came to after the angel freed him from prison, where Herod was holding him to kill him.

John-Mark was also the cousin to Barnabas:

> Aristarchus my fellow prisoner saluteth you, and Marcus
> [Mark], sister's son to Barnabas (Colossians 4:10)

This may explain the contention between Barnabas and Paul that split them up, as recorded in Acts 15. Sometimes family gets in the way of knowing and doing what the will of the Lord is in specific situations. It is very enlightening to understand that men of God make mistakes just like you and I do, as we will see later in Acts.

Something else to consider here is that Mark who wrote the gospel of Mark and Luke who wrote the gospel of Luke and the book of Acts were not of the original twelve apostles of Jesus Christ during His earthly ministry. In their writing of the Word of God, they were described as faithful disciples.

Paul, Barnabas, and John-Mark sailed to Cyprus and docked at Salamis, a Greek city on the east coast of Cyprus. They preached in the synagogue there, crossed the island, and came to Paphos on the southwest coast of Cyprus:

> And when they had gone through the isle unto Paphos,
> they found a certain sorcerer, a false prophet, a Jew,
> whose name was Bar-jesus. Which was with the deputy
> of the country, Sergius Paulus, a prudent man; who
> called for Barnabas and Saul, and desired to hear the
> word of God. But Elymas the sorcerer (for so is his
> name by interpretation) withstood them, seeking to
> turn away the deputy from the faith. Then Saul, (who
> also is called Paul) filled with the Holy Ghost, set his
> eyes on him. And said, O full of all subtilty and all
> mischief, thou child of the devil, thou enemy of all
> righteousness, wilt thou not cease to prevent the right

ways of the Lord? And now, behold, the hand of the Lord is upon thee, and thou shalt be blind, not seeing the sun for a season. And immediately there fell on him a mist and a darkness, and he went about seeking some to lead him by the hand. Then the deputy, when he saw what was done, believed, being astonished at the doctrine of the Lord. Now when Paul and his company loosed from Paphos, they came to Perga in Pamphylia, and John departing from them returned to Jerusalem. (Acts 13:6–13)

What a bold statement by this man of God! Paul called out people who tried to stop God's Word from being spoken. Many Christians today, I believe, would view this as an act of cruelty because Paul did not believe like they do. Stop and take a breath! The man that Paul called out was a sorcerer and false prophet. He was practicing witchcraft, much like witches who try to cast evil spells on a sitting president today. Where was the outrage from the church when that happened? It was basically nonexistent. The end result of a man of God speaking to the evil of his day was that the deputy believed, "being astonished by the doctrine of the Lord."

John-Mark then left Paul and Barnabas and went back to Jerusalem. Paul and Barnabas continued on and came to Antioch in Pisidia, which is in southern Turkey:

But when they departed from Perga, they came to Antioch in Pisida, and went into the synagogue on the sabbath day, and sat down. (Acts 13:14).

The first thing Paul did, as he seemed to do in every town he visited, was go to the synagogue. As usual, he found trouble:

And after the reading of the law and the prophets the rulers of the synagogue sent unto them, saying, ye men and brethren, if ye have any word of exhortation for the people, say on. Then Paul stood up, and beckoning with his hands said, men of Israel, and ye that fear God, give audience. (Acts 13:15–16)

Paul gave a brief history of the time period leading up to Jesus:

The God of this people of Israel chose our fathers, and exalted the people when thy dwelt as strangers in the land of Egypt, and with an high arm brought he them out of it. And about the time of forty years suffered he their manners in the wilderness.... And after that he gave unto them judges about the space of four hundred and fifty years, until Samuel the prophet. And afterward they desired a king, and God gave unto them Saul the son of Cis, a man of the tribe of Benjamin, by the space of forty years. And when he had removed him, he raised up unto them David to be their king, to whom also he gave testimony, and said, I have found David the son of Jesse, a man after mine own heart, which shall fulfill all my will. Of this man's seed hath God according to his promise raised unto Israel a savior, Jesus.... For they that dwell at Jerusalem, and their rulers, because they knew him not, nor yet the voices of the prophets which are read every sabbath day, they have fulfilled them in condemning him. And though they found no cause of death in him, yet desired they Pilate that he should be slain.... But God raised him from the dead.... Be it known unto you therefore, men and brethren, that through this man is preached unto you the forgiveness of sins. And by him all that believe are justified from all things, from which ye could not be justified by the law of Moses. (Acts 13:17–18, 20–23, 27–28, 30, 38–39)

What bold statements Paul made, telling the leaders of the synagogue that they were void of understanding and ignorant of the Word of God that they read every Sabbath day.

Now comes the kicker. If you were to ask how a person gets to heaven, what do you think most people would say? They would tell you to be a good person, not to steal, not to commit adultery, and so forth. Hear the words that the apostle Paul taught: "by Jesus Christ you are justified from all things from which you could not be justified by the Law of Moses." Wow. Later in Acts we see that even the leaders of the church at Jerusalem needed to understand this. It is a tremendous study and an eye-opener.

There will be people who will spread rumors and lie about you. The best thing to do is what Paul did, shake their dust off your feet and walk on:

> And the word of the Lord was published throughout all the region. But the Jews stirred up the devout and honorable women, and the chief men of the city, and raised persecution against Paul and Barnabas, and expelled them out of their coasts. But they shook off the dust of their feet against them, and came to Iconium. (Acts 13:49–51)

They stayed a long time in Iconium, preaching the Word of God:

> And it came to pass in Iconium, that they went both together into the synagogue of the Jews, and so spake, that a great multitude both of the Jews and also of the

Greeks believed. But the unbelieving Jews stirred up the Gentiles, and made their minds evil affected against the brethren. Long time therefore abode they speaking bolding in the Lord, which gave testimony unto the word of his grace, and granted signs and wonders to be done by their hands.… And when there was an assault made both of the Gentiles and also of the Jews with their rulers, to use them despitefully and to stone them. They were aware of it, and fled into Lystra and Derbe cities of Lycoania, and unto the region that lieth round about (Acts 14:1–3, 5–6)

There is a time to walk away and there is a time to stand. We see examples of each in chapter 14. Paul and Barnabas preached in Lystra and healed a man who had been crippled from birth. Because of the power of God that was manifested in Lystra through Paul and Barnabas, the people believed they were gods and wanted to worship them:

And there sat a certain man at Lystra, impotent in his feet, being a cripple from his mother's womb, who never had walked. The same heard Paul speak, who steadfastly beholding him, and perceiving that he had faith to be healed. Said with a loud voice, stand upright on thy feet. And he leaped and walked. And when the people saw what Paul had done, they lifted up their voices, saying in the speech of Lycaonia. The gods are come down to us in the likeness of men. And they called Barnabas Jupiter, and Paul Mercurius, [Mercury] because he was the chief speaker. (Acts 14:8–12)

Now after this notable miracle, can you believe this? The same people from Antioch of Pisidia and Iconium came down to Lystra and stoned Paul, killing him!

> And there came thither certain Jews from Antioch and
> Iconium, who persuaded the people, and having stoned
> Paul, drew him out of the city, supposing he had been
> dead. Howbeit, as the disciples stood round about him,
> he rose up, and came into the city; and the next day he
> departed with Barnabas to Derbe. (Acts 14:19–20)

The disciples used their authority in Jesus Christ and raised Paul
from the dead. Then Paul walked right back into Lystra that same day,
and no man touched him! The minds of the people in Lystra must
have been spinning. Don't you think they knew what had happened to
Paul? They did, and they knew that they had killed him, but Paul and
Barnabas did not walk away. A dead man walking among the people of
Lystra! What a display of the power of God.

After spending the night in Lystra, they preached in Derbe the next
day. They returned back through the same cities where Paul had been
stoned and killed, and where Paul shook off the dust of his feet against
them. This time no man laid a hand on them.

After all that, Paul and Barnabas sailed back to their headquarters
in Antioch of Syria:

> And thence sailed to Antioch, from whence they had
> been recommended to the grace of God for the work
> which they fulfilled.... And there they abode long time
> with the disciples. (Acts 14:26, 28)

While Paul and Barnabas stayed in Antioch of Syria, something
happened that would change the course of how the body of Christ
should function. A great dissension took place among the believers.

CHAPTER 6

The First Council at Jerusalem

Acts 15 starts with an upsetting and confusing statement from Jewish believers in Judaea, who believed that Jesus Christ is the Son of God. They were born again, but they were teaching false doctrines. This was the beginning of division in the church, which is the body of Christ.

Paul, on his first ministry journey, was very clear that belief in Jesus's death, burial, and resurrection was the only way to be justified before God, saved, or born again:

> And certain men which came down from Judaea taught the brethren, and said, except ye be circumcised after the manner of Moses, ye cannot be saved. (Acts 15:1)

These words caused Paul and Barnabas to raise their voices, to put it mildly. These Jewish believers, although sincere, totally misunderstood what Jesus had accomplished for all in this new dispensation of grace. The same damaging heresies are taught today. If you don't do this, you can't be saved; if you don't do that, you can't be saved.

When therefore Paul and Barnabas had no small
dissension and disputation with them, they determined
that Paul and Barnabas, and certain other of them,
should go up to Jerusalem unto the apostles and elders
about this question. (Acts 15:2)

At this point you have to ask. What was being taught in Judaea and
Jerusalem that made those believers confident they were teaching right
doctrine?

When they arrived in Jerusalem, Paul told the apostles and elders
what God had done in their ministry journeys. Sickness was healed,
devils were cast out, and the dead were being raised to life again:

And when they were come to Jerusalem, they were
received of the church, and of the apostles and elders,
and they declared all things that God had done with
them. But there rose up certain of the sect of the
Pharisees which believed saying, that it was needful to
circumcise them, and command them to keep the law
of Moses. (Acts 15:4–5)

The next verse is astounding:
And the apostles and elders came together for to consider
of this matter. (Acts 15: 6)

They did not know what was right. What was the will of God?
Do we have to preform these acts before God to be saved? They either
disregarded or were misinformed about what Paul had been teaching.
Paul, the apostle who received the revelation from Jesus Christ himself,
had been preaching for many years that Christ was the end of the Law.
The apostles and elders were still on a learning curve. Much debate took
place. For sure some fiery words were spoken. Finally, Peter stood up:

And when there had been much disputing Peter rose up
and said unto them, men and brethren, ye know how
that a good while ago God made choice among us, that
the Gentiles by my mouth should hear the word of the
gospel, and believe. (Acts 15:7)

Wow. That says it all. Maybe the apostles had forgotten what Peter
told them when he came back from Cornelius's house in Caesarea. The
Gentiles at Cornelius' house had been saved and gave proof of their
new birth when they heard them speak in tongues and magnify God.
The Gentiles at Cornelius' house were not circumcised and were not
following the Law. The apostles should have been able to put two and
two together. But Peter had to tell them again:

And God, which knoweth the hearts, bare them witness,
giving them the Holy Ghost, even as he did unto us.
(Acts 15: 8)

Then James, the brother of Jesus and the author of the book of
James, spoke. To be clear, James was one of the four brothers of Jesus.

Is not this the carpenter, the son of Mary, the brother
of James, and Joses, and of Juda, and Simon? And are
not his sisters here with us? And they were offended at
him. (Mark 6:3)

He is not to be confused with James the apostle and brother to John
the apostle. Jesus called the two brother apostles, the sons of thunder.

And after they held their peace, James answered, saying,
men and brethren hearken unto me. Simeon [Peter] hath
declared how God at the first did visit the Gentiles, to

take out of them a people for his name. And to this agree the words of the prophets; as it is written.

James then quoted from the book of Amos:

> After this I will return, and will build again the tabernacle of David, which is fallen down; and I will build again the ruins thereof, and I will set it up: That the residue of men might seek after the Lord, and all the Gentiles, upon whom my name is called, saith the Lord, who doeth all these things. (Acts 15:16–17)

The actual words in the book of Amos:

> In that day I will raise up the tabernacle of David that is fallen, and close up the breaches thereof; and I will raise up his ruins, and I will build it as in the days of old. That they may possess the remnant of Edom, and of all the heathen, which are called by my name, saith the Lord that doeth this. (Amos 9:11–12)

The contents of the ninth chapter of Amos is about the thousand-year reign of Jesus Christ on earth; the kingdom age, or the millennial kingdom. This is not to be confused with the church age of grace. Quoting these verses from Amos and attributing them to the grace dispensation, the issue of circumcision, and following the Law is not in the correct time period. It is much like attributing the events that will happen in the book of Revelation and trying to squeeze them in this dispensation of grace.

It was not the time to build again the tabernacle of David that was fallen; that time will come in the millennial kingdom. James, the leader of the church at Jerusalem, was obviously confused about this time period. The apostles were asking the same question the day Jesus ascended into heaven:

> When they therefore were come together, they asked of him, saying, Lord, wilt thou at this time restore again the kingdom to Israel? (Acts 1:6)

James and the other apostles did not yet have the understanding that the rebuilding of the tabernacle of David and the restoration of the kingdom to Israel was not at that time. This is how Jesus answered the apostles' question that day when He ascended into heaven:

> And he said unto them, it is not for you to know the times or the seasons, which the Father hath put in his own power. (Acts 1:7)

Just for clarity, this is how Jesus separated time lines in scripture. One coma in scripture separates a time period of more than two thousand years. Let me explain. This is the scripture Jesus read in his home town Nazareth from the book of Isaiah:

> The spirit of the Lord is upon me, because he hath anointed me to preach the gospel to the poor; he hath sent me to heal the broken hearted, and to preach deliverance to the captives, and recovering of sight to the blind, to set at liberty them that are bruised. To preach the acceptable year of the Lord. (Luke 4: 18-19)

> Jesus stopped in the middle of a sentence and said:

> This day is this scripture fulfilled in your ears. (Luke 4: 21)

If Jesus would have keep reading from Isaiah it would not sync up with the time line of scripture, and Jesus knew it.

This is Isaiah 61:

The spirit of the Lord God is upon me, because the Lord hath anointed me to preach good tidings unto the meek; he hath sent me to bind up the broken hearted, to proclaim liberty to the captives, and the opening of the prison to them that are bound; To proclaim the acceptable year of the Lord, and the day of vengeance of our God. (Isaiah 61: 1-2)

Jesus stopped and did not say "the day of vengeance of our God." Why? His earthly ministry was not in the time line of "the day of vengeance of our God." However, it will be as recorded in Revelation 19: 11-16, and Jesus himself will fulfill it. It is vital to understand the different administrations or time lines in scripture. Jesus gave Paul the responsibility to introduce this administration of grace and the term the body of Christ, which was kept secret from the foundation of the world.

James delivered his judgment:

Wherefore my sentence is, that we trouble not them, which from among the Gentiles are turned to God. (Acts 15:19)

"Wherefore *my* sentence is"? Whenever I read this verse, I have to stop and consider deeply. It seems that James has taken control and is in charge of the church at Jerusalem. It is not my intent to degrade or speak badly about James in any way. However, James is not recognized as an apostle, prophet, or teacher. In the opening statement of the book of James, he declares himself as:

James a servant of God and of the Lord Jesus Christ, to the twelve tribes which are scattered abroad, greetings. (James 1:1).

James was addressing the Jews who were scattered after the stoning of Stephen, which was caused by Paul's persecution of the church:

Now they which were scattered abroad upon the persecution that arose about Stephen travelled as far as Phenice, and Cypras, and Antioch, preaching the word to none but unto the Jews only. (Acts 11:19)

Peter in his epistle addressed the same Jewish believers who were scattered abroad, called the diaspora:

Peter, an apostle of Jesus Christ to the strangers scattered throughout Pontus, Galatia, Cappadocia, Asia, and Bithynia. (1 Peter 1:1)

This was the letter that was drafted by James, the apostles, and the elders, and was sent to the Gentiles in Antioch:

And they wrote letters by them after this manner; the apostles and elders and brethren send greetings unto the brethren which are of the Gentiles in Antioch and Syria and Cilicia. Forasmuch as we have heard, that certain which went out from us have troubled you with words, subverting your souls, saying, ye must be circumcised, and keep the law; to whom we gave no such commandment. It seemed good unto us, being assembled with one accord, to send chosen men unto you with our beloved Barnabas and Paul.... We have sent therefore, Judas and Silas, who shall tell you the same things by mouth. For it seemed good to the Holy Ghost, and to us, to lay upon you no greater burden than these necessary things. That ye abstain from meats offered to idols, and from blood, and from things strangled, and from fornication: from which if you keep yourselves, ye shall do well. Fare ye well. (Acts 15: 23–25, 27–29)

These judgments on what the will of God is was for Gentiles only. The council did not address the Jewish believers; in their minds, nothing had changed. If you were a Jewish believer, you were still required to follow the Law with no exceptions. This was the understanding of James and the apostles, and it was in direct violation of the revelation given to Paul.

We see this demand put upon Paul later in Acts. I believe this is what drove Paul to disregard the prophetic words spoken to him by all the brethren and the prophet Agabus, which ultimately led to his imprisonment.

The truth of the oneness of the body of Christ was not truly recognized, as Paul had been teaching it:

> Therefore by the deeds of the law there shall no flesh be justified in his sight, for by the law is the knowledge of sin. But now the righteousness of God without the law is manifested, being witnessed by the law and the prophets.... Therefore we conclude that a man is justified by faith, without the deeds of the law. (Romans 3:20–21, 28)

There is no separation between Jew and Gentile. Paul's statement applies to both.

This is when a proverbial can of worms begins to open, and the effect of it will be devastating in Paul's life. In Galatians chapter 2,

Paul describes what happened during the discussions at the council in Jerusalem:

> Then fourteen years after I went up again to Jerusalem with Barnabas, and took Titus with me also. And I went up by revelation, and communicated unto them THAT GOSPEL which I preach among the Gentiles, but privately to them which were of reputation, lest by any means I should run, or had run in vain. But neither Titus, who was with me, being a Greek, was compelled be circumcised. (Galatians 2:1–3)

The first thing they wanted to do was to circumcise Titus, but he denied their request. He understood and believed what Paul had been teaching.

> And that because of false brethren unawares brought in, who came in privately to spy out our liberty which we have in Christ Jesus, that they might bring us into bondage. To whom we gave place by subjection, no, not for an hour; that the truth of the gospel might continue with you. But of these who seemed to be somewhat, whatsoever they were, it maketh no matter to me: God accepteth no man's person, for they who seem to be somewhat in conference, added nothing to me. But contrariwise, when they saw the gospel of the uncircumcision was committed unto me, as the gospel of the circumcision was unto Peter.... And when James, Cephas [Peter], and John, who seemed to be pillars, perceived the grace that was given unto me, they gave to me and Barnabas the right hands of fellowship, that

we should go unto the heathen, and they unto the circumcision. (Galatians 2: 4–7, 9)

James, Peter, and John were beginning to understand and perceive the revelation of grace given to Paul. This was not an easy task! Paul talked about false brethren brought in. These were believers in Jesus, they were born again, but they were teaching that believers must follow the Law. This viewpoint is alive and well in churches today!

I do not frustrate the grace of God, for if righteousness come by the law, then Christ is dead in vain. (Galatians 2:21)

The church today needs to stop frustrating the grace of God!

You know that voices were raised and fingers were pointed at this council. Paul was laying it down: "those who seemed to be somewhat in conference added *nothing* to me." Who was Paul talking about here? Who was at this council? The apostles, the elders, John, Peter, and James, the Lord's brother. They seemed to be pillars. It's an interesting phrase that Paul uses.

In other translations: NRSV "those leaders contributed nothing to me" MSG "God isn't impressed with mere appearances, and neither am I. And of course these leaders were able to add nothing to the message I had been preaching"

This council at Jerusalem set the stage for the apostle Paul that later caused so much drama and imprisonment for this great man of God.

When the council was over, Barnabas and Paul returned to Antioch, along with Judas and Silas, who were also prophets:

So when they were dismissed, they came to Antioch, and
when they were gathered, they delivered the epistle....
And Judas and Silas being prophets themselves, exhorted
the brethren with many words, and confirmed them.
(Acts 15:30, 32)

However, the church at Jerusalem was still teaching that the
Jews who believed in Jesus had to continue to follow the Law and be
circumcised. This was a great division in the body of Christ, and still
is today.

CHAPTER 7

The Man of Macedonia

Paul and Barnabas went back to Antioch of Syria, along with Judas and Silas. Sometime after the council at Jerusalem, Peter came to Antioch, and Paul confronted him on a serious issue. The record of this incident between Paul and Peter is recorded in Galatians 2:

> But when Peter was come to Antioch, I withstood him
> to the face, because he was to be blamed. For before that
> certain came from James, he did eat with the Gentiles;
> but when they were come, he withdrew and separated
> himself, fearing them which were of the circumcision.
> (Galatians 2:11–12)

Peter was playing both sides of the fence. He was eating with Gentiles when no Jews were watching, but when James sent other Jews to Antioch, he went into hiding. Peter needed to remember what God had tried to teach him in the vision Peter had on the rooftop. God told Peter not to call any man common or unclean. Did Peter believe Jews were still under the Law? Obviously he did since he hid from the Jews sent by James.

Paul was angry with Peter and had a face-to-face confrontation with him in front of everyone. Whose voice was Peter going to act on? This is the question we all have to answer.

> And the other Jews dissembled likewise with him, [Peter] insomuch that Barnabas also was carried away with their dissimulation. But when I saw that they walked not uprightly according to the truth of the gospel, I said unto Peter before them all, if thou being a Jew, livest after the manner of Gentiles, and not as do the Jews, why compellest thou the Gentiles to live as do the Jews? ... Knowing that a man is not justified by the works of the law, but by the faith of Jesus Christ, even we have believed in Jesus Christ, that we might be justified by the faith of Christ, and not by the works of the law: for by the works of the law shall no flesh be justified. (Galatians 2:13–14, 16)

The Word of God does not tell us what happened after this confrontation. Barnabas also went into hiding with Peter, along with the other Jews. It looks like they all bent the knee and came under the suppression of the Jewish believers sent by James, including Judas and Silas, who were prophets.

Paul and Barnabas came into a serious contention and parted one from another, as I mentioned in a previous chapter. Paul may have been ticked off at Barnabas because Barnabas did not stand his ground and went into hiding with Peter. Similar situations happen today when believers have sharp disagreements about what to do, especially when family is involved. Mark was Barnabas's cousin, and this possibly entered into Barnabas's decision to take Mark with him.

Mark did not finish the first ministry journey with Paul and Barnabas and departed from them in Pamphylia. Paul and Barnabas went their separate ways. The great man of God Barnabas, who was an apostle and prophet, is not mentioned again in the book of Acts:

> And some days after, Paul said unto Barnabas, let us go again and visit our brethren in every city where we have preached the word of the Lord, and see how they do. And Barnabas determined to take with them John, whose surname was Mark. But Paul thought it not good to take him with them, who departed from them from Pamphylia, and went not with them to the work. And the contention was so sharp between them, that they departed asunder one from the other; and so Barnabas took Mark and sailed unto Cyprus. And Paul chose Silas and departed, being recommended by the brethren unto the grace of God. (Acts 15:36–40)

Paul and Silas returned to Derbe and Lystra, where Paul previously was stoned and raised from the dead. At this point, Timothy comes into the picture:

> Then came he to Derbe and Lystra and behold, a certain disciple was there named Timotheus, the son of a certain woman which was a Jewess, and believed, but his father was a Greek…. And as they went through the cities, they delivered them the decrees for to keep, that were ordained of the apostles and elders which were at Jerusalem. (Acts 16:1, 4)

Paul and company went through the cities Phrygia and Galatia, reading the letter written by James. The Holy Ghost at this time forbade them to go to the Far East:

Now when they had gone throughout Phrygia and the region of Galatia, and were forbidden of the Holy Ghost to preach the word in Asia. (Acts 16:6)

So they obeyed, went west and came to Troas. Troas is on the northwestern tip of Asia Minor, what is today called Turkey, on the coast of the Aegean Sea.

And they passing by Mysia came down to Troas. And a vision appeared to Paul in the night, there stood a man of Macedonia, and prayed him, saying, come over into Macedonia and help us. And after he had seen the vision, immediately we endeavoured to go into Macedonia, assuredly gathering that the Lord had called us for to preach the gospel unto them.... And from thence to Philippi, which is the chief city of that part of Macedonia, and a colony, and we were in that city abiding certain days. (Acts 16:8–10, 12)

Arriving at Philippi, they met a woman named Lidia, whose heart the Lord opened when she heard Paul's gospel and believed:

And a certain women named Lidia, a seller of purple of the city of Thyatira, which worshiped God, heard us, whose heart the Lord opened, that she attended unto the things which were spoken of Paul. (Acts 16:14)

Then came an interesting event. As they were going to prayer, a woman possessed by a demonic spirit of divination followed Paul, "saying, these men are the servants of the most high God":

And it came to pass as we came to prayer, a certain damsel possessed with a spirit of divination met with us, which brought her masters much gain by soothsaying. The same followed Paul and us, and cried, saying, these men are the servants of the most high God, which show unto us the way of salvation. (Acts 16:16–17)

What is going on here? The devil was speaking through this woman and telling everybody that what Paul was preaching was true. That does not seem right. People who operate in divination are possessed by evil spirits; make no mistake about that. They come off as the nicest people you would ever meet and tell you words of comfort and support. These are lures that they use to set their hooks in your jaw, teasing you about your future. Psychic hotlines, fortune tellers, thousands of people are taken in by this face of evil that does not look like evil. The devil has many faces; he is not always twisting heads and spitting out green-pea soup. He is very clever.

Paul spoke to the evil spirit, not to the woman:

And this did she many days, but Paul, being grieved, turned and said to the spirit, I command thee in the name of Jesus Christ to come out of her. And he came out the same hour. (Acts 16:18)

This is a manifestation of the Holy Spirit in operation that most Christians do not want to recognize. Most Christians are afraid of the devil and turn tail and run. This is because they have believed movies that make the devil appear more powerful than he is. If you have ever operated in this area and seen it for yourself, all evil spirits have to bow the knee to the name of Jesus Christ.

The men controlling this woman became very angry because they were no longer making money from her so-called talents. Paul cast that evil spirit out. People today finance the devil, and he bleeds them of their money with endless false hopes. It is an endless cycle of insanity.

And when her masters saw that the hope of their gains was gone, they caught Paul and Silas, and drew them into the marketplace unto the rulers. And brought them to the magistrates saying, these men being Jews do exceedingly trouble our city. (Acts 16:19–20)

These men went to the police and made lying accusations against Paul and Silas:

And the multitude rose up together against them, and the magistrates rent off their clothes, and command to beat them. And when they had laid many stripes upon them, they cast them into prison, charging the jailor to keep them safely. Who having received such a charge, thrust them into the inner prison, and made their feet fast in the stocks.(Acts 16:22–24)

Paul and Silas knew they had been sent there by God because of the vision Paul had; so they began to sing and praise God:

And at midnight Paul and Silas prayed, and sang praises unto God: and the prisoners heard them. And suddenly there was a great earthquake, so that the foundations of the prison were shaken, and immediately all the doors were opened, and everyone's bands were loosed. And the keeper of the prison awaking out of his sleep, and seeing the prison doors open, he drew out his sword, and would have killed himself, supposing that the prisoners had been fled. But Paul cried with a loud voice, saying, do thyself no harm, for we are all here. Then he called for a light and sprang in, and came trembling and fell down before Paul and Silas. And brought them out and said, sirs, what must I do to be saved? And they said, believe on the Lord Jesus Christ, and thou shall be saved, and thy house. (Acts 16:25–31)

This jailer was the man of Macedonia whom Paul had seen in his vision, and Paul told him how to be born again. The jailer took them home, cleaned their wounds, and fed them. When the magistrates heard that Paul and Silas were Romans, they wanted to let them go quietly:

> And when it was day, the magistrates sent the serjeants saying, let those men go. And the keeper of the prison told this saying to Paul, the magistrates have sent to let you go; now therefore depart and go in peace. But Paul said unto them, they have beaten us openly uncondemned being Romans, and have cast us into prison, and now do they thrust us out privily? Nay verily, but let them come themselves and fetch us out. And the serjeants told these words unto the magistrates and they feared, when they heard that they were Romans. And they came and besought them, and brought then out, and desired them to depart out of the city. (Acts 16:35–39)

Having been condemned and beaten publicly, there was no way Paul was going to sneak quietly out of town. Paul made those magistrates responsible for their actions. Take note: it is a godly principle. Paul demanded these magistrates come to him publicly and tell him personally. This is a great example of how we as believers should handle certain situations that arise in our lives.

CHAPTER 8

On the Run Again

Paul and company then came to Thessalonica. As was his custom, he went to the synagogue, and for three weeks he taught the Word of God, from Old Testament scripture:

> Now when they had passed through Amphipolis and Apollonia, they came to Thessalonica, where was a synagogue of the Jews. And Paul, as his manner was, went in unto them and three sabbath days reasoned with them out of the scriptures. Opening and alleging that, Christ must needs have suffered, and risen again from the dead, and that this Jesus whom I preach unto you is Christ. (Acts 17:1–3)

What Paul taught is the foundation of Christianity. First, he taught the promised Messiah, who was Jesus, had to suffer and die. Second, the God of Abraham, Isaac, and Jacob raised Him from the dead. Finally, this Jesus was the Christ, the Promised One.

Paul was well educated in the Old Testament, as we call it today. I ask myself, if I only had the Old Testament, could I accurately teach the gospel? Could I prove His death, burial, and resurrection? I would love to have been there to see how Paul made it flow together. Hebrews is a great example of how arguments are presented in comparing how Jesus fulfilled the old covenant.

Some believed what Paul was teaching and some did not. The people who did not believe always lied about him, persecuted him, assaulted him, and even attempted to assassinate him. He was stoned and killed once. What was true back then for Paul is the same thing happening today in our society.

> And some of them believed and consorted with Paul and Silas, and of the devout Greeks a great multitude, and of the chief women not a few. But the Jews which believed not moved with envy, took unto them certain lewd fellows of the baser sort, and gathered a company and set all the city on uproar, and assaulted the house of Jason, and sought to bring them out to the people. And when they found them not, they drew Jason and certain brethren unto the rulers of the city, crying, these that have turned the world upside down are come hither also. Whom Jason hath received: and these all do contrary to the decrees of Caesar, saying that there is another king, Jesus. (Acts 17:4–7)

It only took three weeks (three Sabbath days) for this to happen. This is exactly what is happening today when the name of Jesus is mentioned, especially in the political arena. In Thessalonica they had paid liars, "lewd fellows of the baser sort." When certain lifestyles are confronted with the name of Jesus, you will always see these paid liars on the scene. It got so bad that the brethren had to get Paul and Silas out by night, and they fled to Berea:

And the brethren immediately sent away Paul and Silas by night unto Berea. (Acts 17:10)

These were more noble than those in Thessalonica, in that they received the word with all readiness of mind, and searched the scriptures daily whether those things were so. Therefore many of them believed, also of honorable women which were Greeks, and of the men, not a few. (Acts 17:11–12)

In Berea Paul taught the same truths as he had done in Thessalonica. These Bereans searched the Old Testament, saw it for themselves, and found it to be the truth.

The Jews from Thessalonica, when they heard Paul was preaching in Berea, came after him:

But when the Jews of Thessalonica had knowledge that the word of God was preached of Paul at Berea, they came thither also and stirred up the people. And then immediately the brethren sent away Paul to go as it were to the sea, but Silas and Timotheus abode there still. And they that conducted Paul brought him to Athens, and receiving a commandment unto Silas and Timotheus for to come to him with all speed, they departed. (Acts 17:13–15)

In the Greek city of Athens, Paul saw the temple of Zeus on Mount Olympus, also known as the Acropolis. Paul encountered philosophers of Athens called the Epicureans and the Stoics, and they brought him to Areopagus. The Areopagus is a prominent outcropping rock northwest of the Acropolis. The Areopagus was where the Athenian council met that tried cases of religious and domestic matters. It is also called Mars Hill:

Now while Paul waited for them at Athens, his spirit was stirred in him, when he saw the city wholly given to idolatry. Therefore disputed he in the synagogue with the Jews, and with the devout persons, and in the market daily with them that met with him. Then certain philosophers of the Epicureans and of the Stoicks encountered him. And some said, what will this babbler say? Others said, he seemeth to be a setter forth of strange gods: because he preached unto them Jesus, and the resurrection. And they took him and brought him unto Areopagus, saying, may we know what this new doctrine whereof thou speakest is? For thou bringest certain strange things to our ears, we would know therefore what these things mean. For all the Athenians and strangers which were there, spent their time in nothing else, but either to tell or to hear some new thing. Then Paul stood in the midst of Mars hill, and said, ye men of Athens, I perceive that in all things ye are too superstitious. For as I passed by and beheld your devotions, I found an alter with this inscription, TO THE UNKNOWN GOD. Whom therefore ye ignorantly worship, him declare I unto you. (Acts 17:16–23)

Paul's Acts 17 sermon, on bronze plaque at base of Mars Hill, Athens, Greece. Photo by Leon Mauldin.

What Paul taught at Mars Hill was the mark of a true apostle. In these verses, Paul exposed the truth to these so-called master thinkers, the PhDs of philosophy, as we would say today, who sought after enlightenment. When Paul taught the resurrection from the dead, it was a realm they had never considered. Paul's sermon is encased in a brass plaque at the Areopagus in Athens even today. Written in Greek.

> God that made the world and all things therein, seeing that
> he is Lord of heaven and earth, dwelleth not in temples
> made with hands. Neither is worshiped with mans hands,
> as though he needed anything, seeing he giveth to all life,

and breath, and all things. And hath made of one blood all nations of men for to dwell on all the face of the earth, and hath determined the times before appointed, and the bounds of their habitation. That they should seek the Lord, if haply they might feel after him, and find him, though he be not far from everyone of us. For in him we live and move, and have our being; as certain also of your own poets have said, for we are also his offspring. Forasmuch then as we are the offspring of God, we ought not to think that the Godhead is like unto gold, or silver, or stone, graven by art and man's device. And the times of this ignorance God winked at, but now commandeth all men everywhere to repent. Because he hath appointed a day in the which he will judge the world in righteousness, by that man whom he hath ordained, whereof he hath given assurance unto all men, in that he hath raised him from the dead. And when they heard of the resurrection of the dead, some mocked, and others said, we will hear thee again of this matter. So Paul departed from among them. Howbeit certain men clave unto him, and believed, among the which was Dionysius the Areopagite, and a woman named Damaris, and others with them. (Acts 17:24–34)

Dionysius the Areopagite and a woman called Damaris had to have been astute students of Greek philosophy and the worship of false gods. Yet when they heard the Word of God expounded by Paul, their hearts were changed and moved to the Living God. I don't believe the Athenian council was ever the same after these people were born again. History teaches that Dionysius became a great leader of the believers in Athens, and possibly the first bishop of Athens.

CHAPTER 9

Ephesus and the Elders

Paul left Athens and went to Corinth. He was still in Greece. Corinth is about halfway between Athens and Sparta. There Paul met a married couple named Aquila and Priscilla, who were Jews recently deported from Rome. This deportation took place about AD 53:

> After these things Paul departed from Athens and came to Corinth. And found a certain Jew named Aquila born in Pontus, lately came from Italy, with his wife Priscilla, because that Claudius had commanded all Jews to depart from Rome; and came unto them. (Acts 18:1–2)

Paul was of the same occupation as Aquila and Pricilla, so they worked together in their trade. Paul financed his own way through work:

> And because he was of the same craft, he abode with them and wrought: for by their occupation they were tent makers. (Acts 18:3)

Silas and Timothy arrived in Corinth with Paul and began again testifying to the Jews that Jesus was the Christ:

> And when Silas and Timotheus were come from Macedonia, Paul was pressed in the spirit and testified to the Jews, that Jesus was Christ. And when they opposed themselves and blasphemed, he shook his raiment and said unto them, your blood be upon your own heads, I am clean: from henceforth I will go unto the Gentiles. (Acts 18:5–6)

The Jews in Corinth became more than angry. "They opposed themselves and blasphemed." Their thoughts became insane, and they cursed the name of Jesus that Paul was preaching. However, not all was lost. A man called Justus and another called Crispus, the chief ruler of the synagogue, believed, and many of the Corinthians as well.

We have to understand what was going through Paul's mind at that time. He realized that the Jews were more than angry and were going to come after him, as in the other cities. But the Lord spoke to Paul in a vision by night:

> Then spake the Lord to Paul in the night by a vision, be not afraid, but speak, and hold not thy peace. For I am with thee, and no man shall set on thee to hurt thee: for I have much people in this city. (Acts 18: 9–10)

That must have brought much comfort to Paul and eased his mind:

> And he continued there a year and six months, teaching the word of God among them. And when Gallio was the deputy of Achaia, the Jews made insurrection with one accord against Paul, and brought him to the judgment seat. Saying, this fellow persuadeth men to worship God contrary to the law. (Acts 18:11–13)

Paul was standing at the judgment seat of Gallio. I know what Paul had to be thinking: These men have brought an insurrection against me, and violence is about to erupt. But God said, "No man shall set on thee to hurt thee." God was right on time:

> And when Paul was now about to open his mouth, Gallio said unto the Jews, if it were a matter of wrong or wicked lewdness, O ye Jews, reason would that I should bear with you. But if it be a question of words and names, and of your law, look ye to it, for I will be no judge of such matters. And he drave them from the judgement seat. Then all the Greeks took Sosthenes, the chief ruler of the synagogue, and beat him before the judgement seat. And Gallio cared for none of those things. (Acts 18:14–17)

The tables were turned. Sosthenes, who instigated the insurrection, got the rod across his back, and no man laid a hand on Paul.

> And Paul after this, tarried there yet a good while, and then took his leave of the brethren, and sailed thence into Syria, and with him Priscilla and Aquila. And he came to Ephesus and left them there, but he himself entered into the Synagogue and reasoned with the Jews. (Acts 18:18–19)

Paul moved on to Ephesus with Priscilla and Aquila, but his stay in Ephesus was short this time. He then sailed to Caesarea and came to Antioch in Syria, the headquarters of Paul's ministry. Paul stayed in Antioch some time before he continued his second ministry journey:

> And when he had landed at Caesarea, and gone up, and saluted the church, he went down to Antioch. And after

he had spent some time there, he departed, and went over all the country of Galatia and Phrygia in order to strengthening all the disciples. (Acts 18:22–23)

When Paul returned to Ephesus in Acts 19, I believe it was the highlight of his ministry. This was where he wrote 1 Corinthians. We will see all the special miracles that happened In Ephesus:

And it came to pass, that while Apollos was as at Corinth, Paul having passed through the upper coasts came to Ephesus, and finding certain disciples. He said unto them, have you received the Holy Ghost since you believed? And they said unto him, we have not so much as heard whether there be any Holy Ghost. (Acts 19:1–2)

These men were believers, but they had never heard of the Holy Spirit! Unfortunately this is where most churches are today. Paul's question to them was "have you received the Holy Ghost since you believed?" Obviously, this is the question all believers should ask themselves.

The word *receive* is the key to understanding the question Paul was asking. There are two Greek words dealing with receiving the Holy Spirit that must be understood. These words have different meanings but are both translated as "receive." *Dechomai* means to receive subjectively, within oneself; to be born again. *Lambano* means to receive objectively, to bring it from the inside to the outside or into manifestation.

The Greek word used in the verse where Paul is asking "Have you received the Holy Ghost?" is *lambano*. Paul was asking, have you brought into manifestation the Holy Spirit that is in you since you were born again? Their reply is what is most common today.

"We have not so much as heard whether there be any Holy Ghost" These believers only knew about the baptism of John.

But the manifestation of the spirit is given to every man to profit withal (1 Corinthians 12:7).

Paul laid his hands on them, and they manifested the Holy Spirit by speaking in tongues and prophesying. The laying on of hands is not a requirement to receive the Holy Spirit into manifestation. Remember when Peter went to Cornelius's house, he did not lay his hands on anyone.

> And he said unto them, unto what then were ye baptized? And they said unto John's baptism. Then Paul said, John verily baptized with the baptism of repentance, saying unto the people, that they should believe on him which should come after him, that is on Christ Jesus. (Acts 19:3–4)

Unfortunately, this is as far as most churches go. They get born again, but it stops there.

> And when Paul had laid his hands upon them, the Holy Ghost came on them; and they spake with tongues, and prophesied. And all the men were about twelve. (Acts 19:6–7)

I know there is great controversy about these matters. However, let the Word of God speak for itself:

> If any man think himself to be a prophet, or spiritual, let him acknowledge that the things that I write unto you ARE THE COMMANDMENTS OF THE LORD. But if any man be ignorant, let him be ignorant. Wherefore, brethren, covet to prophesy, and forbid not to speak with tongues. (1 Corinthians 14:37–39)

Paul is very matter-of-fact here. If a man wants to be ignorant, let that man be ignorant. This is the commandment of the Lord. It's your choice!

Don't despise small beginnings. Paul began this great work in Ephesus with twelve men.

Paul taught for more than two years in Ephesus. Great miracles began when he separated the disciples into two groups: those who wanted to believe and follow Paul, and those who wanted to stay ignorant. The separation of believers ignited the special miracles that happened in Ephesus.

> And he went into the synagogue and spake boldly for the space of three months, disputing and persuading the things concerning the kingdom of God. But when divers were hardened, and believed not, but spake evil of that way before the multitude, he departed from them, and separated the disciples disputing daily in the school of one Tyrannus. And this continued by the space of two years; so that all they that dwell in Asia heard the word of the Lord Jesus, both Jews and Greeks. (Acts 19:8–10)

During Paul's time in Ephesus, God brought about special miracles through him:

> And God wrought special miracles by the hands of Paul. So that from his body were brought unto the sick handkerchiefs or aprons, and the diseases departed from them, and the evil spirits went out of them. (Acts 19:11–12)

These cloths, drenched with sweat from his labor as a tentmaker, were taken from his body. Sickness and disease were healed. The very scent of his sweat cast out devils. Do you believe anything like this could happen today? It could if ignorance were abolished in the church. Maybe it starts with separating the disciples, as Paul did in the school of Tyrannus.

The Exorcists

There is always a counterfeit of God's power that tries to steal the scene and divert attention away from God's power to itself. Today, we see politicians, certain religious groups, and governments create crises and then act like they have the solutions. Evil hides behind the things it does by accusing you of doing those same things. It's a smoke screen to divert attention away from themselves. We see this constantly in the political arena.

This is the only place in the Bible where the word "exorcist" is used. An exorcist is one who exercises evil spirits or makes them work for that person. Much like witches do when they cast spells and summons devils, exorcists " exercise" devils to accomplish their tasks.

> Then certain of the vagabond Jews, exorcists, took upon them to call over them which had evil spirits, the name of the Lord Jesus, saying, we adjure you by Jesus whom Paul preacheth. And there were seven sons of one Sceva, a Jew, and chief of the priests, which did so. And the evil spirit answered and said, Jesus I know, and Paul I know, but who are ye? And the man in whom the evil spirit was leaped on them, and overcame them, and prevailed against them, so that they fled out of the house naked and wounded. (Acts 19:13–16)

These Jewish men who were "exorcists" called out an evil spirit in the name of Jesus whom Paul preaches. Who were these men? Seven sons of Sceva, chief of the priests! To get understanding of what's really happening here, we need to go to the prophecy given by Jesus Christ in the gospel of Matthew:

But when the Pharisees heard it, they said, this fellow doth not cast out devils, but by beelzebub the prince of the devils. And Jesus knew their thoughts, and said unto them, every kingdom divided against itself is brought to desolation, and every city or house divided against itself shall not stand. And if satan cast out satan, he is divided against himself, how shall then his kingdom stand? And if I by beeizebub cast out devils, by whom do your children cast them out? Therefore they shall be your judges. (Matthew 12:24–27)

Sceva was the man Jesus was talking to in Matthew 12 who accused Jesus of casting out devils by the prince of devils. Jesus told Sceva that his sons would be his judges. We see this prophecy that Jesus gave come to pass here in Acts 19. Witch doctors operate in this same manner. They use devils to cast out lower-level devils. That makes them look good. It's exciting how the Word of God comes alive. Sceva's sons were doing exactly what Sceva had accused Jesus of. This is how evil hides itself. Jesus knew their thoughts and gave them a lesson on the kingdom of darkness. The kingdom of darkness will not stand because it fights against itself. It will be brought down.

There is a hierarchy in the devil's kingdom. If a general tells a captain to jump, he jumps. But if the captain tells the general to jump, that's a problem. That's what was going on in Acts 19. The seven sons of Sceva were operating with a lower class of devils in the hierarchy, but the evil spirit in this man had a higher ranking. Possibly it was the prince of devils, Beelzebub.

A counterfeit will always try to make itself look genuine. So-called holy water or the showing of a crucifix are nothing more than theatrical stunts. Devils will work in unison to create an image of false reality to secure their identity. It's a facade! Exorcism is the counterfeit for the manifestation of discerning of spirits or casting out devils, as we have seen in Paul's life and as Jesus commanded in the gospel of Mark:

> And these signs shall follow them that believe, in my name shall they cast out devils, and they shall speak with new tongues. (Mark 16:17)

Just for reference, when Jesus said, "they shall speak with new tongues," obviously Jesus was not talking about learned languages or eloquent speech.

After this event with the exorcists, Paul taught the people in Ephesus what had just happened. Fear (respect for the authority of the name of Jesus Christ) and a sense of true repentance came upon them:

> And this was known to all the Jews and Greeks, also dwelling at Ephesus, and fear fell on them all, and the name of the Lord Jesus was magnified. And many that believed came, and confessed, and showed their deeds. Many of them also which used curious arts brought their books together, and burned them before all men, and they counted the price of them and found it fifth thousand pieces of silver. So mightily grew the word of God and prevailed. (Acts 19:17–20)

When these believers at Ephesus really saw the power of God at work, they truly gave up their mixture of curious arts with Christianity. What were these arts? You can still find them in some churches today: crystals, yoga, and paying for prophecy. What deeds did those who confessed at Ephesus show? Curious arts, witchcraft, black magic, white magic or wicca, and the worship of nature. Many believe they are the saviors of the earth that God created. That god like attitude is worshiped in the world today. They burned the books that taught how to cast spells. The people also brought their false gods and burned them. The price of these wicked things was fifty thousand pieces of silver. In today's money, that would be four to five million dollars.

> After these things were ended, Paul purposed in the spirit, when he had passed through Macedonia and Achaia to go to Jerusalem, saying, after I have been there, I must also see Rome. So he sent into Macedonia two of them that ministered to him, Timothous and Eeastus, but he himself stayed in Asia for a season. (Acts 19:21–22)

At the same time, a riot was brewing. A man called Demetrius called a union meeting with his craftsmen because he was losing money. People had stopped buying their false gods. Followers of the way were on the chopping block, including Paul and company:

> And the same time there arose no small stir about that way. For a certain man named Demetrius, a silver smith which made silver shrines for Diana, brought no small gain unto the craftsman. Whom he called together with the workmen of like occupation, and said, sirs, ye know that by this craft we have our wealth. Moreover ye see and hear that not alone at Ephesus, but almost throughout all Asia, this Paul hath persuaded and turned away much people, saying, that there be no gods which are made with hands. So that not only this our craft is in danger to be set at naught; but also that the temple of the great goddess Diana should be despised, and her magnificence should be destroyed, whom all Asia and the world worshippeth. And when they heard these sayings, they were full of wrath, and cried out, saying, great is Diana of the Ephesians. And the whole city was filled with

confusion: and having caught Gaius and Aristarchus, men of Macedonia, Paul's companions in travel, they rushed with one accord into the theatre. And when Paul would have entered in unto the people, the disciples suffered him not. And certain of the chief of Asia, which were his friends sent unto him, desiring that he would not adventure himself into the theatre. (Acts 19:23–31)

The ancient theater at Ephesus

And after the uproar was ceased, Paul called unto him the disciples, and embraced them and departed for to go into Macedonia. And when he had gone over those parts, he had given them much exhortation, he came to Greece. And there abode three months. And when the Jews laid wait for him, as he was about to sail into Syria, he purposed to return through Macedonia. (Acts 20:1–3)

Paul stayed in Greece for three months and wanted to sail on to Syria, but he was informed that those Jews lay in wait to assassinate him. So he changed course and returned through Macedonia. Paul knew the threat to his life; the smell of Paul's blood was in the air. The seven men who accompanied Paul into Asia became his bodyguards.

> And there accompanied him into Asia Sopater of Berea, and of the Thessalonians, Aristarchus and Secundus, and Gaius of Derbe, and Timotheus, and of Asia, Tychicus and Trophimus. These going before tarried for us at Troas. And we sailed away from Philippi after the days of unleavened bread, and came unto them to Troas in five days; where we abode seven days. (Acts 20:4–6)

It was Passover week the days of unleavened bread when Paul sailed from Philippi to Troas. This was a five-day journey, and he stayed in Troas seven days.

> And upon the first day of the week, when the disciples came together to brake bread, Paul preached unto them, ready to depart on the marrow; and continued his speech until midnight. (Acts 20:7)

The subjects that were covered during his speech, I can only imagine: Law and grace, how the manifestations of the Spirit operate, his time in Arabia with Jesus those three years. During Paul's long preaching, a young man was raised from the dead:

> And there sat in a window a certain young man named Eutychus, being fallen into a deep sleep, and as Paul was long preaching, he sunk down with sleep and fell down from the third loft, and was taken up dead. And Paul went down and fell on him, and embracing him said, trouble not yourselves for his life is in him. ...And

they brought the young man alive, and were not a little comforted. (Acts 20:9–10, 12)

I call to mind what Paul wrote in 1 Corinthians. The eyewitnesses of God's power being manifested before all had to be astonishingly miraculous.

And my speech and my preaching was not with enticing words of man's wisdom, but in demonstration of the spirit and of power. (1 Corinthians 2:4)

This is the power that needs to be seen in churches today:

Paul left Troas and walked to Assos, where he was to meet up with his seven bodyguards:

The ancient road from Troas to Assos. Paul walks alone.

And we went before to ship, and sailed unto Assos, there intending to take in Paul; for so he had appointed, minding himself to go afoot. And when he met with us at Assos, we took him in and came to Mitylene. And we sailed thence, and came the next day over against Chios, and the next day we arrived at Samos, and tarried at Trogyllium: and the next day we came to Miletus. For Paul had determined to sail by Ephesus, because he would not spend time in Asia: for he hasted, if it were possible for him to be at Jerusalem the day of Pentecost. (Acts 20:13–16)

Something was stirring in the apostle Paul's life. He walked about twenty miles by himself from Troas to Assos, thinking and praying about what direction he should take. Paul wanted to be in Jerusalem by Pentecost, but he was deeply considering prophetic words that had been spoken to him in other cities by believers, telling him through the spirit not to go in the direction he wanted to go.

And from Miletus he sent to Ephesus, and called the elders of the church. (Acts 20:17)

Paul had just left Ephesus about three and a half months before, but he felt compelled to call the elders to him at Miletus. Why? Prophetic words had been spoken to him through revelation by the elders at Ephesus. He was receiving the same message in every city. What were believers telling Paul? Paul was beginning to justify his actions against what the Spirit of God was speaking to him through the body of Christ.

And when they were come to him, he said unto them, ye know from the first day that I came into Asia, after what manner I have been with you at all seasons. Serving the Lord with all humility of mind, and with many tears, and temptations, which befell me by the lying in wait of the Jews. And how I kept back nothing that was profitable unto you, but have shewed you, and have taught you publickly, and from house to house. Testifying both to Jews and also to the Greeks, repentance toward God, and faith toward our Lord Jesus Christ. (Acts 20:18–21)

Paul reminded the elders of the things he had done and how great those acts were, and they were monumentally miraculous. Paul had spent three years at Ephesus with these believers. He raised up the church there from a start of about twelve men. Obviously these elders of Ephesus gave Paul prophetic words that synced up with other prophetic words that had been given to Paul in every city he went to: "Paul, you should not go to Jerusalem!"

Nevertheless, Paul said:

> And now, behold, I go bound in the spirit unto Jerusalem, not knowing the things that shall befall me there. (Acts 20:22)

Paul went afoot by himself because he was trying to sort out the prophetic words given to him versus his own will. That was why he called the elders of Ephesus. He was driven to go to Jerusalem despite all the revelation he received:

> Save that the Holy Ghost witnesses in every city, saying that bonds and afflictions abide me. (Acts 20:23)

Paul is speaking in past tense, every city he went to were telling him the same things. Repetition of the same prophetic words had to weigh heavy on Paul's mind. Paul apparently made his decision but knew he was bound in the spirit. What does that mean? Have you ever been there? You know you should not do something, but no matter what, you are determined to do it anyway! That's the dilemma Paul was facing in his own life.

So what was his motivation, and what was he going to try to accomplish in Jerusalem? What was going on in Jerusalem that would drive Paul to disregard what the Holy Ghost was witnessing to him? What was going on in Jerusalem? That's the question we should be asking. The Holy Ghost was witnessing to Paul in *every* city, telling him that bad things were going to happen to him in Jerusalem. Paul said:

> But none of these things move me, neither count I my life dear unto myself, so that I might finish my course with joy, and the ministry which I have received of the Lord Jesus, to testify the gospel of the grace of God. And now, behold, I know that ye all, among whom I have gone preaching the kingdom of God, shall see my face no more. (Acts 20:24–25)

Wow! This great man of God was getting weary. He wanted to finish his ministry and die.

Just the other day I saw some statistics concerning ministers and preachers. An astounding percentage have just up and quit or committed suicide. This is the intent of evil, to wear down good people by false accusations and criticism.

Paul endured much more than that. His life was in constant jeopardy. Paul gave his testimony about how bad his trouble was during the time he was in Asia:

> For we would not, brethren, have you ignorant of our trouble which came to us in Asia, that we were pressed out of measure, above strength, insomuch that we despaired even of life. (2 Corinthians 1:8)

This great man of God wanted the apostles and elders at Jerusalem to get in agreement with the revelation Jesus had revealed to him, which applied to both Jew and Gentile. The church at Jerusalem was not teaching that. If you were a Jew, you still had to follow the Law in Jerusalem. Paul believed he could correct this issue.

Paul was reverting to his past, which was forgotten and forgiven. He reminded the elders what he had done when he was a Pharisee, killing and imprisoning believers:

> Wherefore I take you to record this day, that I am pure from the blood of all men … Therefore watch, and remember, that by the space of three years I ceased not to warn everyone night and day with tears.… I have coveted no man's silver or gold or apparel. Yea, ye yourselves know, that these hands have ministered unto my necessities, and to them that were with me. (Acts 20:26, 31, 33–34)

Something monumental was happening. Paul was trying to convince these elders of Ephesus that his decision to go to Jerusalem was justified despite all the prophetic words given to him in every city. Emotions were all over the place! There was intense crying and sobbing as they embraced him with kisses of great respect:

> And when he had thus spoken, he kneeled down, and prayed with them all. And they all wept sore, and fell on Paul's neck and kissed him. Sorrowing most of all for the words which he spake, that they should see his face no more, and they accompanied him unto the ship. (Acts 20:36–38)

This was by far not over yet. God had more in store for Paul. God kept saying the same thing to Paul over and over, using different men and women as messengers, and even a prophet.

CHAPTER 10

On the Road to Jerusalem

After the uproar had ceased, they all had to have been physically and mentally exhausted. We do not know how many elders from Ephesus were there, but there were at least twelve, plus the seven bodyguards traveling with Paul. We can't forget Luke; he was the author of the book of Acts and eyewitness to it all.

Paul and company departed from Miletus and made a straight course through the islands, passing Cyprus on the south side and landing at Tyre:

> And it came to pass that after we were gotten from them, and had launched, we came with a straight course unto Coos, and the day following unto Rhods, and from thence unto Patara. And finding a ship sailing over unto Phenicia, we went aboard and set forth. Now when we had discovered Cyprus, we left it on the left hand, and sailed into Syria, and landed at Tyre: for there the ship was to unlade her burden. And finding disciples we tarried there seven days, who said to Paul through the spirit, that he should not go up to Jerusalem. (Acts 21:1–4)

I have learned from experience that prophetic words spoken to me are often about things God has already been dealing with me about. They are a confirmation of things that God has already spoken. God was trying hard to keep Paul out of trouble. God was talking to the believers through revelation knowledge, trying to get Paul's attention.

Paul stayed in Tyre for seven days, and guess what happened? Paul found disciples, not one disciple but many. Many times a day, believers would have prophesied to him words of knowledge and wisdom by the spirit, saying, "Paul, you should not go up to Jerusalem!" At this point it was a no-brainer what Paul should be doing.

Paul believed he had a mission at Jerusalem, but whatever mission he saw was not being sanctioned by God. Paul was struggling in his own will. This drive to disregard all was astonishing!

After Tyre, they came to Ptolemais and stayed one day. Then they went to Caesarea and stayed with Philip the evangelist, who was one of the seven. What did it mean to be one of the seven? Back in Acts chapter 6, the apostles handed over a business that ministered to the believers, and chose seven men to run it. Philip was one of them. Stephen the martyr was also one of the seven:

> Wherefore brethren, look ye out among you seven men of honest report, full of the Holy Ghost and wisdom, whom we may appoint over this business. But we will give ourselves continually to prayer, and to the ministry of the word. And the saying pleased the whole multitude: and they chose Stephen, a man full of faith and of the Holy Ghost, and Philip, and Prochorus, and Nicanor, and Timon, and Parmenas, and Nicolas a proselyte of Antioch. (Acts 6:3–5)

Philip knew Stephen very well. Paul was the man who had consented to Stephen's death and had had him stoned. Paul and company stayed at Philip's house.

> And the next day we that were of Paul's company departed, and came to Caesarea: and we entered into the house of Philip the evangelist, which was one of the seven, and abode with him. And the same man had four daughters, virgins, which did prophesy. (Acts 21:8–9)

Philip had four daughters who prophesied. What do you think they prophesied about? They no doubt prophesied about what the whole context of this part of God's Word talks about: Paul going to Jerusalem. The four daughters of Philip prophesied the same things the disciples in Tyre and the elders at Ephesus did. In every city that Paul went to, believers were saying the same things: "Paul, you should not go up to Jerusalem!"

What came next was God's final attempt to get through to Paul. God used a tried-and-true prophet whose name was Agabus. He was the same prophet who had prophesied the famine that came to pass in the days of Claudius Caesar (see chapter 5).

> And as we tarried there [at Philip's house] many days, there came down from Judaea a certain prophet, named Agabus. And when he was come unto us, he took Paul's girdle, and bound his own hands and feet, and said, THUS SAID THE HOLY GHOST, so shall the Jews at Jerusalem bind the man that owneth this girdle, and shall deliver him into the hands of the Gentiles. (Acts 21:10–11)

When Agabus arrived, the first thing he did was to take Paul's girdle. Paul's girdle was a strip of cloth that held his long garment at the waist, similar to a belt. Agabus did not ask permission; he took Paul's girdle forcefully. Agabus lay on the ground and tied his own hands and feet. He looked directly into Paul's eyes with authority and said, "THUS SAID THE HOLY GHOST."

Notice the word "shall" in these verses. It is an absolute. It was used to get Paul's attention, to make it clear that what Agabus was saying was from the throne of the almighty God and the Lord Jesus Christ.

This was a dramatic scene. The seven men that accompanied Paul, Philip and all his house and Agabus the prophet witnessed this dramatic scene. The seven men heard all the prophetic words spoken to Paul from Troas to Philip's house. Timothy was one of those seven men. This group of believers tried their best to persuade Paul not to go to Jerusalem, but to no avail. After all that was said and done, what did they all say to Paul?

> And when we heard these things, both we, and they
> of that place, besought him not to go up to Jerusalem.
> (Acts 21:12)

This was the absolute will of God for Paul's life. How did Paul answer? It was not good.

Something was going on in Paul's mind. He wanted to be in Jerusalem at Pentecost. He knew all of the apostles and elders would be there. Pentecost was one of the three feast days when Jews had to show up at the Temple in Jerusalem. Paul said to Agabus and the others:

> Then Paul answered, what mean ye to weep and to
> break mine heart? For I am ready to not be bound only,
> but also to die at Jerusalem for the name of the Lord
> Jesus. (Acts 21:13)

This was not what God was calling Paul to do. I have heard ministers and preachers teach this passage of scripture as motivation. Paul was ready to die for the gospel! If they really understood what was happing here, they would never use this passage as motivation in that way. Paul was outside of God's will! He was dead wrong! So what was driving his compulsion to ignore the Spirit of God that had been spoken to him over and over and over again.

Paul knew what was going on in Jerusalem. Because of his love for his brethren, the Jews in Jerusalem, he believed he could fix the problem. What was the problem? The problem that had not been addressed in the council at Jerusalem in Acts 15. Believing Jews were still doing all the Law as worship to God. This whole thing was about to unfold. At the end of this painful and dramatic scene, they stopped pleading with Paul:

> And when he would not be persuaded, we ceased, saying, the will of the Lord be done. (Acts 21:14)

Paul, you know what the will of the Lord is. Please just do the will of the Lord! *Don't go to Jerusalem!*

CHAPTER 11

Paul Goes to Jerusalem

After this event at Philip's house, Paul and his seven companions got their belongings together and headed toward Jerusalem:

> And after those days we took up our carriages, and went up to Jerusalem. There went with us also certain of the disciples of Caesarea, and brought with them one Mnason of Cyprus, an old disciple with whom we should lodge. And when we were come to Jerusalem, the brethren received us gladly. (Acts 21:15–17)

That last verse should arrest your attention. Why? For months all that Paul had heard in every city he went to was, "don't go to Jerusalem." But the brethren in Jerusalem were glad to see Paul. What a contrast! This should give us a hint of the spiritual temperature in Jerusalem.

On the next day, Paul and company went to see James, the Lord's brother, and the elders:

> And the day following Paul went in with us unto James, and the elders were present. And when he had saluted them,

he declared particularly what things God had wrought among the Gentiles by his ministry. (Acts 21:18–19)

Paul saluted them and talked particularly of what God had done through his ministry among the Gentiles. Possibly about the young man that Paul had raised from the dead just weeks before. All the miracles that had taken place in Ephesus, where devils were cast out by the scent of Paul's sweat just months ago.

The next verse begins to tell the story of what was going on in Jerusalem. Can you imagine? After hearing about all the miracles and manifestations of God's power, they were interested in one thing:

And when they heard it, they glorified the Lord, and said unto him. Thou seest, brother, how many thousands of Jews there are which believe, and they are all zealous of the law. (Acts 21:20)

What does it mean to be "zealous of the law"? All believing Jews continued to practice Mosaic Law as part of their duty, and worship of God. That included animal sacrifice for sin and purification practices to show they were approved before God. This was happening in Jerusalem among all believing Jews, elders and apostles included. This is where most of the churches are today, preforming for God by doing their religious services as part of their righteousness and justification. Some go so far as to say; this must be done to maintain your salvation.

James said to Paul:
And they are informed of thee, that thou teachest all the Jews which are among the Gentiles to forsake Moses, saying, that they ought not to circumcise their children, neither to walk after the customs. What is it therefore?

The multitude must needs come together: for they will hear that thou art come. (Acts 21:21–22)

James was asking Paul, "What is it therefore?" Why are you doing this? Paul had been teaching for years that Christ was the end of the Law and that circumcision was of the heart and not of the flesh. The first council at Jerusalem had dealt with Gentiles only, saying that they did not have to follow the Law or be circumcised. However, the church at Jerusalem and their leaders kept practicing the Law as if it was still fulfilling a requirement from God. Paul's going to Jerusalem was to help them comprehend that Jesus had fulfilled all of the Law, and the Law's practices were ended and obsolete. To continue to offer anything for sin had become an idol:

> For he is not a Jew which is one outwardly, neither is circumcision, which is outward in the flesh. But he is a Jew, which is one inwardly, and circumcision is of the heart, in the spirit, and not in the letter, whose praise is not of men, but of God. (Romans 2:28–29)

James demanded that Paul fall in line, walk in an orderly fashion, and keep the Law:

> "Do therefore this that we say to thee."

This was not a request but a demand. This was an order! Paul had been healing the sick, raising the dead, and casting out devils, but the apostles and elders at Jerusalem were concerned only that Paul follow the Law. Does that remind you of similar things happening today in some churches?

> Do therefore this that we say to thee: we have four men which have a vow on them. Them take, and purify

thyself with them, and be at charges with them, that they may shave their heads, and all may know that those things, wherefore they were informed concerning thee, ARE NOTHING: But that thou thyself also walkest orderly, and KEEPEST THE LAW. (Acts 21:23–24)

Let's break down the order given to Paul by James, the elders, and the apostles:

- *Purify thyself.* What does that involve? Animal sacrifice for sin and more. Numbers 6 describes what Paul was expected to do. They obviously believed Paul was in sin, because they expected him to make an offering for sin.
- *Be at charges with them.* They demanded that Paul pay for lamb and ram offerings for the four men and himself. Cakes of fine flour mingled with oil also had to be provided by Paul. This had to be done to prove to James and company that what Paul was teaching was nothing.
- *Walk orderly and keep the law.* Going forward, Paul could not step out of line again. He had to keep the Law.

This was exactly why God had tried to keep Paul out of this mess. This was God's problem, not Paul's. Approximately in twelve years, God would deal with this problem. Paul's imprisonment took place in Jerusalem in AD 57 to 58. The Temple in Jerusalem would be destroyed by the Romans in AD 70. This was God's statement to both believing and unbelieving Jews. What are you going to do now, seeing there is no more Temple? The sacrifice for sin has already been made. Get your doctrine in line with what I revealed to Paul the apostle.

Paul's love for his brethren had motivated him in the wrong direction. His good intentions had gone astray. Freedom is a precious thing. God did not want Paul to fall into the hands of the state, the Roman empire, the Gentiles. Unfortunately it happened.

James now refreshed Paul's memory about what had taken place in Jerusalem during the first council, seven to eight years previously:

> As touching the Gentiles which believe, we have written and concluded that they observe NO SUCH THING, save only that they keep themselves from things offered to idols, and from blood, and from strangled, and from fornication. (Acts 21:25)

What such thing was that? Circumcision and the Law. There had been no change for believing Jews; they still believed they were required by God to follow all the Law. That was exactly what the church at Jerusalem was teaching for believing Jews. So we can we conclude that the church at Jerusalem was teaching that the body of Christ had two different ways of serving God. The Jewish believers had to follow the Law, but the Gentile believers did not. What a mess that was, ignoring the dispensation of grace given to Paul by Jesus Christ himself.

This is the division we see in many churches today in many different forms. What idol or temple has to be destroyed in our understanding so that the simplicity of Christ is understood through Paul's gospel?

> Behold Israel after the flesh: are not they which eat of the sacrifices partakers of the alter? What say I then? that the idol is anything. (1 Corinthians 10:18–19)

> The Temple and the sacrifices became the idol, just as the brazen serpent that Moses made to heal the children of Israel became an idol. King Hezekiah had to destroy that brazen serpent just like the temple had to be destroyed. See 2 Kings 18.

Once I understood this whole concept it opened doors of new understanding. Spiritual authority needs to be respected and honored not worshiped.

There were also slanderous reports of Paul teaching grace as a license to sin:

> For if the truth of God hath more abounded through my lie unto his glory, why yet am I also judged as a sinner? And not rather, as we be slanderously reported, and as some affirm that we say, let us do evil that good may come. (Romans 3:7–8)

Who was there on Pentecost when Paul was called out for this grievous offense? James and all the elders, including the apostles.

The epistle 2 Corinthians was written by Paul about AD 57 or 58, possibly during the same year Paul came to Jerusalem. There was conflict between the church at Jerusalem and Paul. It was no different from what we see today in the denominations of churches.

> For we dare not make ourselves of the number, or compare ourselves with some that commend themselves, but they measuring themselves by themselves, and comparing themselves among themselves, are not wise. (2 Corinthians 10:12)

> For I suppose, I was not a whit behind the chiefest apostles. (2 Corinthians 11:5)

> For in nothing am I behind the very chiefest apostles, though I be nothing. (2 Corinthians 12:11)

Paul's teachings and authority were challenged by slanderous reports. Paul was willing to go through this process. He believed he could bring the light to his brethren that Jesus was the fulfillment of all the Law by His death, burial, and resurrection. No further action would be required.

The revelation of the body of Christ was revealed to Paul by Jesus Christ Himself during Paul's three years in Arabia. But it was still a foreign doctrine to the church at Jerusalem, and it was extremely hard for Paul to break through the walls of their tradition:

> If ye have heard of the dispensation of the grace of God which is given to me, to you-ward. How that by revelation he made known unto me the mystery; as I wrote afore in few words. Whereby, when ye read, ye may understand my knowledge in the mystery of Christ. Which in other ages was not made known unto the sons of men, as it is now revealed unto his holy apostles and prophets by the spirit. That the Gentiles should be fellow heirs, and of the same body, and partakers of his promise in Christ by my gospel. (Ephesians 3:2–6)

> For there is no difference between the Jew and the Greek. (Romans 10:12)

Gentiles had one set of rules and Jews had a different set of rules. Paul knew this was not God's will. Abuse of the grace of God was taking place.

> For if the blood of bulls and of goats and calves, and the ashes of an heifer sprinkling the unclean, sanctifieth to the purifying of the flesh. How much more shall the blood of Christ, who through the eternal spirit offered himself without spot to God, purge your conscience from dead works to serve the living God? (Hebrews 9:13–14)

It is still a great controversy today, dead works of the Law versus grace. Today's controversy does not manifest in the same way the Jews at Jerusalem were confronted. We don't have controversy about sacrificing animals for sins; it's more covert and deceptive.

Then came the crushing blow to the great apostle Paul. Paul was willing to pacify their demands in hope of opening their eyes to the truth of the gospel that Jesus had revealed to him. The seven-day purification process that Paul performed by order of James was almost at the end, when Jews from Asia saw him and proceeded to kill Paul:

> Then Paul took the men, and the next day purifying himself with them entered into the temple, to signify the accomplishment of the days of purification, until that an offering should be offered for every one of them. And when the seven days were almost ended, the Jews which were of Asia, when they saw him in the temple, stirred up all the people, and laid hands on him. Crying out, men of Israel, help: this is the man that teacheth all men every where against the people, and the law, and this place: and further brought Greeks also into the temple, and hath polluted this holy place.... And all the city was moved, and the people ran together: and they took Paul, and drew him out of the temple, and forthwith the doors were shut. And as they went about to kill him, tidings came unto the chief captain of the band, that all Jerusalem was in an uproar. Who immediately took soldiers and centurions, and ran down unto them: and when they saw the chief captain and the soldiers, they left beating of Paul. Then the chief captain came near, and took him, and commanded him to be bound with two chains, and demanded who he was, and what he had done. (Acts 21:26–28, 30–33)

Thus came about the fulfillment of all the prophetic words given to Paul, including the final word from the prophet Agabus. From this time on, Paul was a prisoner of the Roman Empire and no longer free. This was not God's will for Paul.

CHAPTER 12

The Imprisonment

Paul was held captive by the Roman Empire. He was on the defensive,
trying to justify himself to a mob that was trying to kill him:

> And when he came upon the stairs, so it was, that he
> was borne of the soldiers for the violence of the people.
> For the multitude of the people followed after, crying,
> away with him. (Acts 21:35–36).

Paul begins his defense with a history of himself to this mob. How
he put to death followers of the way, and what happened to him on the
road to Damascus:

> Men, brethren, and fathers, hear ye my defense which
> I make now unto you.... I am verily a man which am a
> Jew, born in Tarsus, a city in Cilicia, yet brought up in
> this city at the feet of Gamaliel, and taught according
> to the perfect manner of the law of the fathers, and
> was zealous toward God, as ye all are this day. And
> I persecuted this way unto the death, binding and

delivering into prisons both men and women.... And it came to pass, that, as I made my journey, and come neigh to Damascus about noon, suddenly there shone from heaven a great light round about me. And I fell unto the ground and heard a voice saying unto me, Saul, Saul, why persecutest thou me? And I answered. Who art thou Lord? And he said unto me, I am Jesus of Nazareth, whom thou persecutest.... And I said, what shall I do Lord? And the Lord said unto me, arise, and go unto Damascus; and there it shall be told thee of all things which are appointed for thee to do.... And one Ananias, a devout man according to the law, having a good report of all the Jews which dwelt there. Came unto me and stood, and said unto me, brother Saul, receive thy sight. And the same hour I looked up upon him.... For thou shall be his witness unto all men of what thou hast seen and heard. ... And it came to pass, that when I was come again to Jerusalem, even while I prayed in the temple, I was in a trance. And saw him saying unto me, make hast, and get thee quickly out of Jerusalem: for they will not receive thy testimony concerning me. (Acts 22:1, 3–4, 6–8, 10, 12–13, 15, 17–18)

Things had not changed! Paul's testimonial speech fell on deaf ears, and the smell of Paul's blood was in the air:

And they gave him audience unto this word, and then lifted up their voices, and said, away with such a fellow from the earth, for it is not fit that he should live. And as they cried out, and cast off their clothes, and threw dust into the air. (Acts 22:22–23)

The chief captain, seeing that extreme violence was about to erupt, brought Paul into the castle. They were going to interrogate Paul by severe beatings, but stopped when Paul claimed his Roman citizenship:

> The chief captain commanded him to be brought into the castle, and bade that he should be examined by scourging: that he might know wherefore they cried so against him. And as they bound him with thongs, Paul said unto the centurion that stood by, is it lawful for you to scourge a man that is a Roman, and uncondemned? … Then straightway they departed from him which should have examined him, and the chief captain was also afraid, after he knew that he was a Roman, and because he had bound him. (Acts 22:24–25, 29)

The Next Day

After the violent acts and accusations calmed down somewhat, the Roman guards brought Paul to the high priest and the council, who were accusing him. Paul began speaking, saying he had a good conscience before God. The high priest did not even let him finish and commanded that Paul be struck across his mouth:

> On the marrow, because he would have known the certainty wherefore he was accused of the Jews, he loosed him from his bands, and commanded the chief priest and all their council to appear, and brought Paul down, and set him before them. And Paul earnestly beholding the council, said, men and brethren, I have lived in all good conscience before God until this day. And the high priest Ananias commanded them that stood by him to smite him on the mouth. Then Paul said unto him, God shall smite thee, thou whited

wall: for sitttest thou to judge me after the law, and commandest me to be smitten contrary to the law? (Acts 22:30, 23:1–3)

"Whited wall?" What does that mean? Let's get a good definition from Jesus:

> Woe unto you, scribes and Pharisees, hypocrites! For ye are like unto whited sepulchers, which indeed appear beautiful outward, but are within full of dead men's bones, and of all uncleanness. (Matthew 23:27)

"Whited wall" refers to a grave site. The entrance to a grave or sepulcher was whitewashed to make it look good, but what was inside was dead men's bones. Ananias, a high priest, was the father-in-law of the high priest Caiaphas, who had soldiers strike Jesus across His mouth after He was taken prisoner from the garden of Gethsemane.

Paul next used his wits and made an attempt to divide the council, which was made up of Pharisees and Sadducees. Pharisees believed in the resurrection of the dead. Sadducees did not believe in the resurrection of the dead or in any spiritual life.

> But when Paul perceived that the one part were Sadducees, and the other Pharisees, he cried out in the council, men and brethren, I am a Pharisees, the son of a Pharisees, of the hope and resurrection of the dead, I am called in question. And when he had so said, there arose a dissension between the Pharisees and the Sadducees: and the multitude was divided. For the Sadducees say that there is no resurrection, neither angel, nor spirit, but the Pharisees confess both. And there arose a great cry, and the scribes that were of the Pharisees part, arose

and strove, saying, we find no evil in this man: but if
a spirit or an angel hath spoken to him, let us not fight
against God. And when there arose a great dissension,
the chief captain fearing lest Paul should have been
pulled in pieces of them, commanded the soldiers to go
down, and take him by force from among them, and to
bring him into the castle. (Acts 23:6–10)

What a skirmish! They were pushing and pulling at Paul, so the
soldiers got Paul out before he was pulled to pieces. Then Jesus came
to Paul the following night and spoke to him:

And the night following the Lord stood by him, and
said: Be of good cheer, Paul: for as thou hast testified
of me in Jerusalem, so must thou bear witness also at
Rome. (Acts 23:11)

The fight to kill Paul was by no means over. The Jews made an
ingenious plot. More than forty men bound themselves under a curse.
These men vowed not to eat or drink anything until they killed Paul.
The next day they made a plan to kill Paul by lying to the chief captain.

And when it was day, certain of the Jews banded
together, and bound themselves under a curse, saying
that they would neither eat or drink till they had killed
Paul. And they were more than forty which had made
this conspiracy. And they came to the chief priests and
elders, and said, we have bound ourselves under a great
curse, that we will eat nothing until we have slain Paul.
Now therefore ye with the council signify to the chief
captain that he bring him down unto you tomorrow,
as though ye would inquire something more perfect

concerning him: and we, or ever he come near, we are ready to kill him. (Acts 23:12–15)

It had been three days since Paul was taken prisoner in the Temple, and no one had spoken up or tried to intervene for him. Where was everybody? Was political correctness alive back then as it is today? It took a courageous boy, Paul's sister's son, to start the process of helping Paul. This boy heard the plot to kill his uncle, went to the castle, and informed Paul.

> And when Paul's sister's son heard of their lie in wait, he went and entered into the castle, and told Paul. Then Paul called one of the centurions unto him, and said, bring this young man unto the chief captain, for he hath a certain thing to tell him..... Then the chief captain took him by the hand, and went with him aside privately, and asked him, what is it that thou hast to tell me. And he said, the Jews have agreed to desire thee that thou wouldest bring Paul down tomorrow into the council, as though they would inquire somewhat of him more perfectly. But do not thou yield unto them, for there lie in wait for him of them more than forty men, which have bound themselves with an oath, that they will neither eat or drink till they have killed him: and now are they ready, looking for a promise from thee. (Acts 23:16–17, 19–21)

The chief captain understood the severity of this threat and immediately had two centurions make ready to leave Jerusalem with Paul. The threat of assassination was so severe, they had to take Paul out under cover of night. Even at night the chief captain ordered four hundred and seventy Roman soldiers to ensure Paul's safety.

So the chief captain then let the young man depart, and charged him, see thou tell no man that thou hast showed these things to me. And he called unto him two centurions, saying, make ready two hundred soldiers to go to Caesarea, and horsemen threescore and ten, and spearmen two hundred, at the third hour of the night. And provide beasts that they may set Paul on, and bring him safe unto Felix the governor. (Acts 23:22–24)

CHAPTER 13

Two Years in Caesarea

Paul and his escort of Roman soldiers stopped at Antipatris, a town built by Herod the Great and most likely named after his father, Antipater. It was the halfway point between Jerusalem and Caesarea:

> Then the soldiers, as it was commanded them, took Paul and brought him by night to Antipatris. On the morrow they left the horsemen to go with him, and returned to the castle. Who, when they came to Caesarea, and delivered the epistle to the governor, presented Paul also before him.… I will hear thee, said he, when thine accusers are also come, and he commanded him to be kept in Herod's judgement hall. (Acts 23:31–33, 35)

The high priest Ananias and the elders were extremely angry that Paul had slipped through their fingers:

> And after five days, Ananias the high priest decended with the elders, and with a certain orator named Tertullus, who informed the governor against Paul.

And when he was called forth, Tertullus began to accuse him, saying, seeing that by thee we enjoy great quietness, and that very worthy deeds are done unto this nation by thy providence.... For we have found this man a pestilent fellow, and a mover of sedition among all the Jews throughout the world, and a ringleader of the sect of the Nazarenes ... But the chief captain Lysias came upon us, and with great violence took him away out of our hands. (Acts 24:1–2, 5, 7)

Paul was then given permission to speak by Felix:

But this I confess unto thee, that after the way which they call heresy, so worship I the God of my fathers, believing all things which are written in the law and prophets.... And herein do I exercise myself, to have always a conscience void of offense toward God, and toward men. (Acts 24:14, 16)

What a profound statement from the apostle Paul. After all he'd been through, he exercised his conscience to be without offense. Offense is a cancer that destroys from the inside out, if allowed. What a great attribute Paul demonstrated in his life, taking control of his thoughts. He rendered his "conscience void of offence, toward God and man."

At this time we need to pause and consider what this great man, the apostle Paul, endured. Not all of the trials Paul endured are recorded in the book of Acts:

Of the Jews five times received I forty stripes save one. Thrice was I beaten with rods, once was I stoned, thrice I suffered shipwreck, a night and a day I have been in the deep: In journeyings often, in perils of water, in perils of robbers, in perils by mine own countrymen, in perils by the heathen, in perils in the city, in perils in the wilderness, in perils in the sea, in perils among false brethren: In weariness and painfulness, in watchings often, in hunger and thirst, in fastings often, in cold and nakedness. Beside those things that are without, that which cometh upon me daily, the care of all the churches. (2 Corinthians 11:24–28)

And when Felix heard these things, having more perfect knowledge of that way, he deferred them, and said, when Lysias the chief captain shall come down, I will know the uttermost of your matter. (Acts 24:22)

The chief priest and elders did not like the way Felix handled the situation with Paul. Felix gave Paul liberty and allowed acquaintances to visit him. However, it is not recorded that anybody came to Paul during those two years in Caesarea. Felix spent a lot of time with Paul during those two years:

And he commanded a centurion to keep Paul, and to let him have liberty, and that he should forbid none of his acquaintance to minister or come unto him. And after certain days, when Felix came with his wife Drusilla, which was a Jewess, he sent for Paul, and heard him concerning the faith of Christ. And as he reasoned of righteousness, temperance, and judgement to come, Felix trembled, and answered, go thy way for this time; when I have a convenient season I will call for thee. He hoped also that money should have been given him of Paul, that he might loose him: wherefore he sent for him oftener, and communed with him. (Acts 24:23–26)

Drusilla was the daughter of Herod Agrippa, the man who had ordered James the apostle to be killed. Felix was hoping someone would pay for Paul's release, but no one came. According to some historical documents, Ananias the high priest made formal complaints against Felix and Lysias, demanding of the Roman authorities that they be replaced. Stating that peace in Jerusalem was being compromised by the way Felix handled this prisoner Paul.

At the end of two years, Felix was replaced by Porcius Festus by order of Nero:

> But after two years Porcius Festus came into Felix' room. (Acts 24:27)

At this point Festus took over as governor in the province of Judea.

Festus spent three days in Caesarea with Felix, being informed of everything that had transpired in the last two years concerning Paul. Festus then traveled to Jerusalem to meet with these Jews who were accusing Paul:

> Now when Festus was come into the province, after three days he ascended from Caesarea to Jerusalem. Then the high priest and the chief of the Jews informed him against Paul, and besought him. And desired favor against him, that he would send for him to Jerusalem, laying wait in the way to kill him. But Festus answered, that Paul should be kept at Caesarea, and that he himself would depart shortly. Let them therefore, said he, which among you are able, go down with me, and accuse this man, if there be any wickedness in him.... And when he was come, the Jews which came down from Jerusalem stood round about, and laid many and grievous complaints against Paul, which they could not prove. (Acts 25:1–5, 7)

In the next verse, Paul made the decision to be judged in Rome. He knew if he were brought back to Jerusalem, that would mean certain death. The curse those forty men put upon themselves was still in play. Paul would be assassinated! Paul remembered what Jesus spoke to him the second night after he was taken prisoner in Jerusalem:

> Be of good cheer Paul, for as thou hast testified of me in Jerusalem, so must thou bear witness also at Rome. (Acts 23:11)

> But Festus, willing to do the Jews pleasure, answered Paul, and said, wilt thou go up to Jerusalem, and there be judged of these things before me? Then said Paul, I stand at Caesar's judgement seat, where I ought to be judged, to the Jews have I done no wrong, as thou very well knowest. For if I be an offender, or have committed anything worthy of death, I refuse not to die; but if there be none of these things whereof these accuse me, no man may deliver me unto them, I appeal unto Caesar. (Acts 25:9–11)

After some days, King Agrippa came to Caesarea to congratulate Festus on his new position and to see how things were going. King Agrippa was the son of Herod Agrippa, who killed the apostle James. King Agrippa and Festus had a long talk about the prisoner Paul. Festus had found no fault in Paul and did not know what to write to Nero about Paul's crimes. Festus knew the political pressure on him, so he asked King Agrippa for assistance:

> But when I found that he had committed nothing worthy of death, and that he himself hath appealed to Augustus [Nero Claudius Caesar Augustus Germanicus was Nero's

full name], I have determined to send him. Of whom I have no certain thing to write unto my lord. Wherefore I have brought him forth before you, and specially before thee O king Agrippa, that, after examination had, I might have somewhat to write. For it seemed to me unreasonable to send a prisoner, and not withal signify the crimes laid against him. (Acts 25:25–27)

Paul was brought before King Agrippa. Paul began the account of his life with his training as a Pharisee in Jerusalem, and how he did many things against the believers and made them blaspheme the name of Jesus of Nazareth:

And I punished them often in every synagogue, and compelled them to blaspheme, and being exceeding mad against them, I persecuted them even unto strange cities. (Acts 26:11)

Paul continued with his Damascus experience and the purpose of his life, and stated what he was teaching:

That Christ should suffer, and that he should be the first that should rise from the dead, and should shew light unto the people, and to the Gentiles. (Acts 26:23)

Festus had some choice words for Paul:

And as he thus spake for himself, Festus said with a loud voice, Paul, thou art beside thyself; much learning doth make thee mad. But he said, I am not mad most noble Festus, but speak forth the words of truth and soberness. (Acts 26:24–25)

These were the last words Paul spoke to King Agrippa:

> For the king knoweth of these things, before whom also
> I speak freely: For I am persuaded that none of these
> things are hidden from him, for this thing was not done
> in a corner. King Agrippa, believest thou the prophets?
> I know that thou believest. Then Agrippa said unto
> Paul, almost thou persuadest me to be a christian. ….
> And when he had thus spoken, the king rose up, and
> the governor, and Bernice, and they that sat with them.
> And when they were gone aside, they talked between
> themselves, saying, this man doeth nothing worthy
> of death or of bonds. Then said Agrippa unto Festus,
> this man might have been set at liberty, if he had not
> appealed unto Caesar. (Acts 26:26–28, 30–32)

CHAPTER 14

On the Road to Rome

Paul was destined to be sent to Rome, Italy. It became a wild ride of typhoons, shipwrecks, and snake bites. He had another believer with him,

> Aristarchus, my fellow prisoner, of Thessalonica. (Colossians 4:10)

> And when it was determined that we should sail into Italy, they delivered Paul and certain other prisoners unto one named Julius, a centurion of Augustus' band. And entering into a ship of Adramyttium, we launched, meaning to sail by the coasts of Asia; Aristarchus, a Macedonian of Thessalonica, being with us. And the next day we touched at Sidon, and Julius courteously entreated Paul, and gave him liberty to go unto his friends to refresh himself. (Acts 27:1–3)

Julius, the centurion in charge of the prisoners, must have been instructed either by Festus or King Agrippa to take care of Paul and treat him right. The care that was given to Paul was not the norm for prisoners.

And when we had sailed over the sea of Cilica and
Pamphylia, we came to Myra a city of Lycia. And there
the centurion found a ship of Alexandria sailing into
Italy, and he put us therein. (Acts 27:5–6)

Paul and the other prisoners were transferred to a larger ship sailing
to Italy. The number of persons aboard this larger ship was two hundred
and seventy-six. Traditionally these ships transported wheat from
Alexandria in Egypt to Italy. According to other studies, these ships
were 140 feet long and 37 feet wide.

And we had sailed slowed many days, and scarce were
come over against Cnidus, the wind not suffering us, we
sailed under Crete, over against Salmone: And, hardly
passing it, came unto a place which is called the fair havens,
neigh whereunto was the city of Lasea. Now when much
time was spent, and when sailing was now dangerous,
because the fast was now already past, Paul admonished
them. And said unto them, sirs, I perceive that this voyage
will be with hurt and much damage, not only of the lading
and ship, but also of our lives. Nevertheless the centurion
believed the master and the owner of the ship, more than
those things which were spoken by Paul. (Acts 27:7–11)

Paul knew it was dangerous to sail during this season. The feast
of the Day of Atonement had already passed, which occurs in late
September. The owner of the ship did not listen to Paul because a
smooth southern wind began to blow. The owner believed he was
making the right decision and set sail:

And when a south wind blew softly, supposing that they
had obtained their purpose, loosing thence, they sailed

close by Crete. But not long after there arose against it a tempestuous wind, called Eurocyldon. (Acts 27:13–14)

They were in the middle of a typhoon, the perfect storm:

> And when the ship was caught, and could not bear up into the wind, we let her drive.… And we being exceedingly tossed with the tempest, the next day they lightened the ship. And the third day we cast out with our own hands the tackling of the ship. And when neither sun nor stars in many days appeared, and no small tempest lay on us, all hope that we should be saved was then taken away. (Acts 27:15, 18–20)

Paul reminded them that they should have listened to him. But he also said,

However, I have good news. An angel of God appeared to me. It's going to be OK:

> But after long abstinence, Paul stood forth in the midst of them, and said, sirs, ye should have hearkened unto me, and not have loosed from Crete, and to have gained this harm and loss. And now I exhort you to be of good cheer, for there shall be no loss of any man's life among you, but of the ship. For there stood by me this night the angel of God, who's I am, and whom I serve. Saying, fear not Paul, thou must be brought before Caesar: and lo, God hath given thee all them that sail with thee. Wherefore sirs, be of good cheer, for I believe God! That it shall be even as it was told me. Howbeit we must be cast upon a certain island. (Acts 27:21–26)

At the time Paul spoke these words, they had been in the storm for about five days. On the fourteenth day things began to change. The storm seemed to take on strength:

> But when the fourteenth night was come, as we were driven up and down in Adria [the Adriatic Sea], about midnight the shipmen deemed that they drew near to some country. And sounded, and found it twenty fathoms, and when they had gone a little further, they sounded again, and found it fifteen fathoms. Then fearing lest we should have fallen upon rocks, they cast four anchors out of the stern, and wished for the day..... Paul said to the centurion and to the soldiers, expect these abide in the ship, ye cannot be saved. And while the day was coming on, Paul besought them all to take meat, saying, this day is the fourteenth day that ye have tarried and continued fasting, having taken nothing. (Acts 27:27–29, 31–33)

What took place next was astounding. The two hundred and seventy-six souls on board the ship had not eaten for fourteen days. I imagine their bellies were not in the best shape. Paul gave thanks and broke bread in the presence of them all, a form of communion service:

> Wherefore I pray you to take some meat, for this is for your health, for there shall not an hair fall from the head of any of you. And when he had thus spoken, he took bread and gave thanks to God in presence of them all, and when he had broken it, he began to eat. Then were they all of good cheer, and they also took some meat. And we were in all in the ship two hundred threescore and sixteen souls. And when they had eaten enough,

they lightened the ship, and cast out the wheat into the sea. And when it was day, they knew not the land: but they discovered a certain creek with a shore, into the which they were minded if it were possible to thrust in the ship.… And falling into a place were two seas met, they ran the ship aground, and the forepart stuck fast, and remained unmoveable, but the hinder part was broken with the violence of the waves. And the soldiers' council was to kill the prisoners, lest any of them should swim out, and escape. But the centurion willing to save Paul, kept them from their purpose, and commanded that they which could swim should cast themselves first into the sea, and get to land. And the rest some on boards, and some on broken pieces of the ship. And so it came to pass, that they escaped all safe to land. (Acts 27:34–39, 41–44)

Was that not a wild ride for Paul and company? And this was not Paul's first shipwreck! He states in Corinthians that he survived two other shipwrecks, though they are not recorded in the book of Acts:

Thrice I was shipwrecked, a night and a day I have been the deep (2 Corinthians 11: 25)

Three Months on the Island of Melita:
Paul was on the final leg of his journey to Rome. He had been through a typhoon and a shipwreck. A snake bite would be next:

And when they were escaped, then they knew that the island was called Melita. And the barbarous people shewed us no little kindness, for they kindled a fire and received us every one, because of the present rain, and because of the cold. And when Paul had gathered a bundle of sticks, and laid them on the fire, there came a viper out of the heat and fastened on his hand. And when the barbarians saw the venomous beast hang on his hand, they said among themselves, no doubt this man is a murderer, whom though he hath escaped the sea, yet vengeance suffereth him not to live. And he shook off the beast into the fire, and felt no harm. Howbeit they looked when he should have swollen or fallen down dead suddenly, but after they had looked a great while, and saw no harm come to him, they changed their minds, and said that he was a god. (Acts 28:1–6)

These island people knew that snake was very poisonous. When God's power is manifested, it will change minds:

In the same quarters were possessions of the chief man of the island, who's name was Publius; who received us, and lodged us three days courteously. And it came to pass, that the father of Publius lay sick of a fever and of a bloody flux, to whom Paul entered in and prayed, and laid his hands on him, and healed him. So when this was done, others also, which had diseases in the island, came and were healed. Who also honoured us with many honours, and when we departed, they laded us with such things as were necessary. And after three months we departed in a ship of Alexandria, which had wintered in the isle who sign was Castor and Pollux. (Acts 28:7–11)

Paul left the island of Melita with the gratitude and thankfulness of the island people. All who came to Paul were healed of sickness and disease. The island people would never forget those three months.

Paul's Entrance into Rome:

The new ship took Paul and company to Syracuse, a city on the southeastern coast of Sicily, where they stayed three days. Then they sailed to Rhegium on the southernmost tip of the mainland of Italy. Another day of sailing brought them to Puteoli, where they found brethren and stayed seven days. That was the last seaport for Paul, who continued on foot to Rome:

> And landing at Syracuse, we tarried there three days. And from thence we fetched a compass, and came to Rhegium: and after one day the south wind blew, and we came the next day to Puteoli. Where we found brethren, and were desired to tarry with them seven days, and so we went toward Rome. (Acts 28:12–14)

Puteoli was a great seaport where large ships unloaded grain for Rome. The road from Puteoli to Rome was called the Appian Way. When Paul entered Rome, he was not sent with the other prisoners, but was allowed to dwell by himself with a soldier. The favorable treatment of Paul continued:

> And when we came to Rome, the centurion delivered the prisoners to the captain of the guard, but Paul was suffered to dwell by himself with a soldier that kept him. And it came to pass, that after three days Paul called the chief of the Jews together, and when they came together, he said unto them, men and brethren, though I have committed nothing against the people,

or customs of our fathers, yet was I delivered prisoner from Jerusalem into the hands of the Romans.... And they said unto him, we neither received letters out of Judea concerning thee, neither any of the brethren that came shewed or spake any harm of thee. But we desire to hear of thee what thou thinkest: for as concerning this sect, we know that everywhere it is spoken against. (Acts 28:16–17, 21–22)

The same thing happened to Paul that had happened every place he had been some believed and some didn't:

And when they had appointed him a day, there came many to him into his lodging, to whom he expounded and testified the kingdom of God, persuading them concerning Jesus, both out of the law of Moses, and out of the prophets, from morning till evening. And some believed the things which were spoken, and some believed not.... Saying, go unto this people, and say, hearing ye shall hear, and shall not understand, and seeing ye shall see, and not perceive. For the heart of this people is waxed gross, and their ears are dull of hearing, and their eyes have they closed, lest they should see with their eyes, and hear with their ears, and understand with their heart, and should be converted, and I should heal them.

These were the last two years of the apostle Paul living in his own rented house. He taught the Word of God in Rome. No man stopped him from speaking the truth about the Lord Jesus Christ. During the last years of Paul's life in Rome he penned most of the New

Testament: Ephesians, Philippians, Colossians, 1 and 2 Timothy, Titus, and Philemon.

> And Paul dwelt two whole years in his own hired house, and received all that came in unto him. Preaching the kingdom of God, and teaching those things which concern the Lord Jesus Christ, with all confidence, no man forbidding him. (Acts 28:30)

The Conclusion and the Epistle to the Hebrews:

In these last two years of Paul's life, he wrote to Timothy and other epistles to the churches. From the time Paul fell prisoner to the Romans in Jerusalem to his time in Rome, the believers began to digress. The churches in Asia began to repudiate the authority of Paul's gospel. It was a very sad situation.

Paul wrote to Timothy:

> This thou knowest, that all they which are in Asia be turned away from me. (2 Timothy 1:15)

The erosion began through lying rumors and vicious attacks on Paul and his gospel. John the apostle wrote about what was happening in the churches in the late first century. The epistle of 3 John was written about AD 90, some twenty-plus years after Paul's death in Rome.

> I wrote unto the church: but Diotrephes, who loved to have the preeminence among them, received us not. Wherefore, if I come, I will remember his deeds which he doeth, prating against us with malicious words: and not content therewith, neither doth he himself receive the brethren, and forbiddeth them that would, and casteth them out of the church. (3 John 1: 9–10)

The forming of religion was beginning to happen. Unauthorized leaders were taking authority and dominance over the churches. This was the direct result of the rejection of the dispensation of the gospel of grace that Jesus Christ revealed to Paul.

The book of Hebrews is all about the sacrifice of Jesus Christ's body, which fulfilled all of the Law of Moses. The author of Hebrews has been somewhat hidden for various reasons.

Paul was the apostle to the Gentiles; that was his calling. However, the first place Paul went whenever he entered a city was the synagogue. When we read Hebrews, you can almost hear the arguments Paul had with believing and unbelieving Jews.

Paul penned in great detail what the Law could not do anymore, believing that his writings would fall on the ears of the church in Jerusalem. Paul was the apostle to the Gentiles. He did not want to trespass on another's responsibility:

> Yea, so have I strived to preach the gospel, not where Christ was named, lest I should build upon another man's foundation. (Romans 15:20)

This was the responsibility of the apostle to the circumcision. Paul did not pen his name on the book of Hebrews like he did on his other letters for that reason.

The last verses of Hebrews give some insight into who penned this wonderful book:

> And I beseech you, brethren, suffer the words of exhortation, for I have written a letter unto you in few words. (Hebrews 13:22)

"Suffer the words of exhortation" is rendered in other translations as "I urge you to bear with my words," "pay attention to my words," and "listen patiently to my words." The statement, "for I have written a letter unto you in few words" makes me laugh. Hebrews is one of the longest books in the New Testament.

> Know ye that our brother Timothy is set at liberty, with
> whom, if he come shortly, I will see you. (Hebrews 13:21)

Timothy was Paul's spiritual son in the faith. If anybody was going to send Timothy, it was Paul.

> Salute all them that have the rule over you, and all the
> saints, they of Italy salute you. (Hebrews 13:24)

There is no doubt that Hebrews was written by Paul during his last two years in Rome, Italy.

One last statement from the apostle Paul that I hope will help you remember who this man was, and his heart toward people and Jesus Christ the Lord. This is how he walked in love even if it was not reciprocated.

> And I will very gladly spend and be spent for you,
> though the more abundantly I love you, the less I be
> loved. (2 Corinthians 12:15)

Pat's Poem in a Psalm:

Around the two years of one
Heavens breath blew again on the land
With it's soul intent to bring a soul for all the souls in
the land
And heavens breath blew
And there now stands a man that will always stand with
you

Printed in the United States
by Baker & Taylor Publisher Services